G000138686

FAMILY ON MISSION

CELEBRATING 25 YEARS OF *BRINGING
HOPE, HELP AND HEALING*
AT DROP INN

Family on Mission
Copyright © 2019 Neil Dawson
ISBN: 978-1-9162332-0-1

All rights reserved.
No part of this publication may be reproduced, stored in a retrieval system, or transmitted in any form or by any means, electronic, mechanical, photocopying or otherwise, without prior written consent of the publisher except as provided by under United Kingdom copyright law. Short extracts may be used for review purposes with credits given.

All Scriptures quoted are taken from New King James Version, except where stated. Scripture taken from the New King James Version®; Copyright © 1982 by Thomas Nelson. Used by permission. All rights reserved.

Scripture quotations taken from The Authorized (King James) Version. Rights in the Authorized Version in the United Kingdom are vested in the Crown. Reproduced by permission of the Crown's patentee, Cambridge University Press.

THE HOLY BIBLE, NEW INTERNATIONAL VERSION®, NIV® Copyright © 1973, 1978, 1984, 2011 by Biblica, Inc.® Used by permission. All rights reserved worldwide.

Scripture quotations marked MSG are taken from *THE MESSAGE*, copyright © 1993, 2002, 2018 by Eugene H. Peterson. Used by permission of NavPress. All rights reserved. Represented by Tyndale House Publishers, Inc.

Scripture quotations marked NLT are taken from the *Holy Bible*, New Living Translation, copyright © 1996, 2004, 2015 by Tyndale House Foundation. Used by permission of Tyndale House Publishers, Inc., Carol Stream, Illinois 60188. All rights reserved.

The Christian Standard Bible. Copyright © 2017 by Holman Bible Publishers. Used by permission. Christian Standard Bible®, and CSB® are federally registered trademarks of Holman Bible Publishers, all rights reserved.

Published by
Maurice Wylie Media
City Life Centre
143 Northumberland Street
Belfast
Northern Ireland
BT13 2JF (UK)

Publishers' statement: *Throughout this book the love for our God is such that whenever we refer to Him we honour with Capitals. On the other hand, when referring to the devil, we refuse to acknowledge him with any honour to the point of violating grammatical rule and withholding capitalisation.*

For more information visit
www.MauriceWylieMedia.com

ENDORSEMENTS

"For me, the most inspiring people in life are those who give Jesus their wholehearted YES, no matter what it costs or where it could lead them. Ronnie and Carolyn Dawson and their family have said YES to Jesus on countless occasions over the last 25 years, counting it all joy. despite the many secret sacrifices. The result is the transformation, physically, emotionally, and spiritually, of thousands of people in multiple nations for the glory of God! Their remarkable story will inspire you towards the rollercoaster ride of life in all its fullness when you start with that wholehearted, full-throated YES to Jesus Christ."
Alain Emerson
Lead Pastor, Emmanuel Church, Lurgan, Northern Ireland.

"It has been our great privilege to have partnered with Drop Inn ministries for almost all of their 25 years. I love their heart for mission, both at home and overseas, inspired by Ronnie and Carolyn and the team. In the true spirit of Jesus, the Good News has been preached, captives have been released and the broken have been made whole. Lives have been changed forever! I am believing for many more Good News stories in years to come because legacy has been built into the ministry."
Michael Rollo
Senior Leader, Found Church, Larbert, Scotland.

"In reading the stories within the story of Drop Inn, I am challenged to see the profound journey that came from asking the question; 'What do we do?' The ingrained value of being family and walking together makes Drop Inn an inspirational story in bringing hope, help and healing to a hurting world. We have so much to learn: a must-read!
Malini Colville
Home for Good - Northern Ireland Lead.

"This is not only the story of a 'Family on Mission,' but it is actually the story of the Kingdom of God. Our Abba Father has employed the family paradigm as the model for His Kingdom. The early Apostles did the same, and this was the pattern Paul worked from in his church and missionary ministry. God's Kingdom is a family business and He extends His business across the world through His sons and daughters. Truly, the Kingdom moves at the pace of relationships. The Kingdom will not spread or even function properly without the Father/Son relationship: first with God and then with each other. It is time for the church to move from institutionalised structures to family ties, and ministry must turn from professionalism to parental love: fathers and mothers raising sons and daughters. This is the wonderful testimony of a remarkable family which embodies this Kingdom reality. It has not just revolutionised their own natural family, but the family of God across the globe. Many will rise up and call them blessed!"
David Legge
Bible teacher and author, Northern Ireland.

"Do you believe in miracles? Whether you do or not, reading the story of Drop Inn ministries will leave you with no doubt that the last 25 years have been nothing less than miraculous. From a simple step of obedience of one couple in Richhill, Northern Ireland, a ministry has grown that has impacted the lives of tens of thousands in numerous nations of the world. This truly is an inspirational story of hope, help and healing."

Tommy Stewart
Director, Christians Who Lead, Ballymena, Northern Ireland.

"The experiences I had as a young person travelling through Eastern Europe with Drop Inn changed the trajectory of my life in profound and meaningful ways. Exposed to poverty, challenged to push beyond my 'entitled' comfort zones and being caught up in the Dawson family's extraordinary vision to exercise the Great Commission and bring the masses along on the journey, captivated my heart and demonstrated the necessity of laying down your life to conformity and instead daring to dream big, impactful dreams. This is the story and the legacy of the Dawson family. I can honestly say, this family's dream for mission and justice catalysed me to dream about a better world, where the Kingdom of kindness breaks in and lives are changed in simple and beautiful ways. I am forever thankful to have surfed in the wake of these pioneers!"

Laura Wylie
CEO, Links Counselling Service, Northern Ireland.

FOREWORD

It was in 2002, when a young man entered our church in Lurgan, Northern Ireland and began worshipping with us. I could sense immediately that there was something significant in his life: it was evident that he had a hunger and a passion for God.

Neil Dawson, the author of this book, would become one of those people that I simply did life with and I've loved the friendship that ensued. We released him in 2005 to plant a church alongside his dad, Ronnie, in Richhill; and even though he was no longer part of our congregation, our friendship continued to grow and strengthen.

I remember when I first met Neil. He reminded me of Timothy in the Scriptures. He was teachable and hungry to learn, always eager to step out into the deep, and into the journey God has taken him on from then to now. I've loved seeing it unfold!

The apostle Paul refers to Timothy as his 'son in the faith;' then later on refers to Timothy as his 'brother in the ministry.' That's a bit like what I feel about Neil; these young men are sons who become brothers in ministry.

This book is a tribute to Neil's parents, Ronnie and Carolyn, and the journey of Drop Inn ministries over the last quarter of a century: bringing hope, help and healing to a hurting world.

It's so easy to look at the vastness of the world's issues or even our local communities' issues and do nothing because we feel overwhelmed. Not so with Ronnie Dawson. His heart was caught by the many and one by one in his local community of Richhill, he began to make a difference.

Watching the young people of his community who were sliding down the slippery slope of drugs and alcohol, he knew he couldn't just be an observer or passer-by. Running onto the pitch, Ronnie became a key player in their lives. But while his little home town of Richhill was the original plan for the mission, after some disasters around the world, Ronnie's spiritual antenna went up; and he headed for Europe with a truck load of aid.

This developed into many regular such trips and then later the work developed into the opening of the well-known Drop Inn thrift shops which raise money to support the work right across Europe.

Today, there are shops across Northern Ireland, the Isle of Man and the USA. Birthed from the little village of Richhill, these shops provide revenue that now service over 20 countries around the globe. Pretty impressive, I think!

Of course, we know work like this can't be done alone, and Ronnie's wife Carolyn is also a key player in this ministry. Carolyn is one of the most hospitable ladies that I am privileged to know. She reminds me much of my own Mum who is now in Glory. They are the type of people who make everyone feel as if they belong and that they are special. Carolyn also makes the best carrot cake in the whole world!

Over the last fifteen years or so I have had the tremendous privilege to be known as a friend of Ronnie and Carolyn Dawson. I know that both of them could never have believed where this road would take them; but even with all that happened, both were willing to sacrifice and obey the call to step out and follow the promptings and leading of the Holy Spirit.

We would all love it if God would give us a map of our lives; but in my experience, as with Ronnie and Carolyn, God seems to be more into compasses than maps! He points a way for us to go and if we are smart, we should go!

Ronnie and Carolyn did just that: like Abraham of old, when God pointed a direction without giving Abraham any foreknowledge of where it might lead him. Moses was directed back to Egypt after forty years with no idea of how he would be received or what the outcome would be. Yet these men did exactly what Ronnie and Carolyn Dawson did twenty-five years ago: they trusted themselves into the hands of a God who loved them; and the rest is history!

This book that you now have in your hands will reveal the many highs and lows they encountered along the way.

In closing, let me say a few words which sum up Ronnie and Carolyn... commitment; longevity; stickability; faithful; loving; generous; and powerfully sacrificial.

*I am truly honoured to serve in the Kingdom alongside men and women like the Dawsons, and I know that their journey as a **Family on Mission** continues.*

Love and Prayers,
Pastor Phil Emerson,
Senior Pastor, Emmanuel Church, Lurgan, Northern Ireland.

CONTENTS

INTRODUCTION

Setting the scene...

I have written this book to explain the story of my family, the sacrifices that have been made and the impact that a willing heart can have in the nations. If you live in Northern Ireland, you'll probably know my family best through our charity shops called Drop Inn.

We started off in humble beginnings in a little village called Richhill, Co Armagh, Northern Ireland, growing to 30 shops throughout the province, and with shops in the Republic of Ireland, Isle of Man and America. We also own the Tin House coffee shop in Portadown.

I have loved partnering with people across the nations, to hear stories of how the resources and support that we have been fortunate enough to supply them with have changed their communities. It is truly inspirational and humbling. I really want to acknowledge these brave people who have stepped up and decided to make a difference in their local areas. Our lives have really become intertwined with these pioneers. All these places that were once just little dots on a map, seemingly insignificant to me at the time; now, when I step back and look at the bigger picture, the impact is amazing!

I want to honour the sacrifice and investment my parents initiated and I want to highlight those who have been impacted by that. The reality is, because of the work they have done, people have been empowered across different nations to change communities and to have great influence with those around them in powerful ways. It has really shown me that when we partner with Kingdom-minded people, anything is possible!

This had a huge impact on me as a young boy growing up in the *Dawson* household. It helped to increase my own personal faith, showing me how powerful God is and that He is at work around the world. No one is insignificant to Him, no matter how small they may appear on a world map!

The work of Drop Inn ministries is God-centred and relational. God has called us to love others. To love one another is essential to fulfil the Great Commission: We are highly committed to doing so in our lives; hopefully we encourage others around us to do the same. Jesus said; *'As the father has sent me, so I am sending you.'* (John 20:21)

A few years later, Paul reminds us; *'We are His Ambassadors, as though Jesus was making his appeal through us.'* (2 Corinthians 5:20)

As followers of Jesus, we are truly representing the *family* business, which is to see all people reconciled to God. Reconciled as sons and daughters created in the image of Father God. In the formative years of Drop Inn, the lyrics of the *Casting Crowns* song, '*If we are the Body*,' became like an anthem for us:

"But if we are the body... Why aren't His arms reaching?
Why aren't His hands healing? Why aren't His words teaching?
And if we are the body... Why aren't His feet going?
Why is His love not showing them there is a way?"

As a son, I want to demonstrate how God called, stretched and led my parents and friends to follow Him, to love those around them and to share stories that are a consequence of saying '*yes*' over and over again.

As a father myself, it grieves me how quickly a generation '*turns from the way of their fathers.*' When I read chapters like Deuteronomy 6, I find myself paying close attention. This Scripture is a reminder to the children of Israel of how they were rescued, who they are to love and what is promised to them. The call on their lives was that through them, all the nations of the world would be blessed. Their call was so counter-cultural that, as verse 20 says, sons will ask; '*What is the meaning of all that God has asked of us?*' Then fathers would go back to the beginning of their story and tell the next generation of how they were rescued, and the journey of discovering the reason why they were rescued. (v21-23) Today, even my own children are asking questions; "*Dad, why do our lives look like this? Why are our priorities so different from those around us?*"

3

In Joshua chapter four, it tells us that after 40 years of wandering in the desert, Joshua, in succession to Moses, leads the children of Israel across the Jordan River into the land of promise. After the whole nation has crossed over, God tells Joshua to choose 12 men, one from each tribe, to carry a stone from the middle of the river; *'these stones would be a permanent memorial for the people of Israel.'* (Joshua 4:7) As God tells Joshua, we should set up something visible so that in the future your kids will ask; *'What do these stones mean?'* When they ask, point them to how I was always with you.

These were thoughts that often went through my mind growing up, as I became aware of how my life was different from my friends' lives. Now I want to live in such a way that carries on that same legacy; that provokes those same thoughts. I want those who have inspired this story to remember God's faithfulness; I want the generation that follows me to be familiar with His goodness.

Eugene Peterson's 'Message' translation of Psalms 78:2-4 helps sum up my motivation for sharing this story;

"Stories we heard from our Fathers counsel, we learned at our mother's knee. We're not keeping this to ourselves, we're passing it along to the next generation, God's fame and fortune, the marvellous things he has done."

'I was afraid I might disappoint you so I did nothing.'
Matthew 25:24-26 MSG

(paraphrased)

I pray this would never be said of us...

CHAPTER ONE

Responding to the call...

To set the scene of this story I will take you back to the late Seventies to when my parents first met. My mum often tells me that she had a very ordinary, but happy and carefree childhood. Her parents, both Christians, were heavily involved in the local church and ensured that Mum and her five sisters were there as often as possible! It was years later that Mum realised what a privilege it had been to grow up in a church environment and, like me, she is so grateful for the Godly influence on her life from an early age.

When my mum was thirteen, she gave her life to Jesus at an after-church coffee bar which was run by her older sister, Pauline and husband Billy. It was here, a few years later when my mum was about sixteen, a young man, whose parents were friends of the family, came into her life. Having recently rededicated his life to Jesus, Ronnie Dawson was looking for Christian friends and started hanging out with the youth group.

My dad, Ronnie, hadn't always been fully engaged with the Lord in his youth. However, after being involved in a very serious motorbike accident at the age of seventeen, he started to refocus his life. It was this near-death experience that had him reconnect with God. Unfortunately, one of the problems he had at that time was that he had no Christian friends. Dad and his friends were only interested in motorbikes and girls! He knew that in order to succeed spiritually, he needed to connect with others his own age who were committed to following God.

After hearing about the youth group in Armagh, he decided to visit. He found that they were very proactive in their worship, their prayer and outreach. This is not only where he developed a deep relationship with the Lord; but also where he met the love of his life! Deciding to attend the youth centre was a decision that had a huge impact on the direction of his life in more ways than one!

After a while, despite a few ups and downs, my parents started dating and became engaged on Mum's 18th birthday. Dad didn't waste any time, though, and just one year later, on 5th June 1982, they were married in Markethill Elim Church. They had planned to be married in their local church in Armagh; but just a few months before their big day, the church had been badly damaged when a bomb had gone off in a nearby building. Unfortunately, that was just the 'norm' of living in Northern Ireland at that time!

My dad was twenty-one and my mum was only nineteen when they got married. On their wedding day, they were given a promise; 'In all your ways acknowledge him and he will direct your path,' Proverbs 3:6 NKJV. As a young married couple, they decided that this Scripture would become their motto in life. From that day on, in all their plans and decisions they would include God. They sought God and prayed about everything together as a couple. It was a great platform as they set out in their lives together.

The church had always played a significant role in both their lives. So, in 1982, when my grandad Joe Dawson planted an Elim Church in Richhill, they joined him and my Granny Florence, eager and ready to serve. My parents decided to put their names down for a house in the area, so they could be a support to them. For the first few years of their married life, they were involved in all aspects of the church in the Richhill community.

Most of you who'll read this book won't have ventured through the beautiful village of Richhill. In fact, the majority of you have probably never even heard of it! Richhill is a small rural village in County Armagh, Northern Ireland, situated between the town of Portadown and the capital, Armagh. It has a small friendly population of just over 3,000 people. There is a great sense of community. This was where my parents began their happy marriage, while becoming part of the Richhill village community.

Two years later, on 31st August 1984, I entered the world. My mum to this day often jokes about me being such a laid-back person, as 11 days after her due date, she was still awaiting my arrival! Two years later, my sister Nicola was born and so our little family was complete. As far as my mum is concerned, we were and continue to be her most precious gifts from God. My mum, Carolyn, was a stay-at-home mum and a childminder. She supported my dad through all the stages of the ministry, but remained at home raising us until we were both seventeen and independent. Now today things are very different: my parents minister together and never seem to be more than 10 feet apart!

With my dad serving alongside my grandfather in church leadership, Sunday school was very normal for me and my sister

Nicola. One time my dad, mum, sister and I were on our way to our local holiday resort of Portrush for a family holiday. During that car ride, I had the privilege of leading my little sis to the Lord.

Our childhoods were quite *normal* and uneventful. With Richhill being a sleepy village, nothing much really happens in and around it, just typical village life. All the drama of the larger towns happened outside this. I still recall something that happened when I was about ten years old: one morning my Dad was sitting at the kitchen table reading the local newspaper and the front page was quite memorable. In the Ulster Gazette, the front headline story was *all about* Richhill! This had to be a first! Usually it would have been stories about the other surrounding towns but not this time: Richhill had hit the headlines!

Sadly, the headlines were not good. The story was all about the drugs and alcohol abuse happening in our small village. It was shocking at that time! This front page really caught my dad's attention. Little did he know it, but this was going to signify a huge turning-point; not only in *his* life but in the lives of many others!

The headline read... '**Anti-social behaviour in Richhill Park!**' I remember that he put the paper down and said to my mum; "*What are we going to do about this?*"

As Believers, then, we must be Jesus' representatives; and in being His representatives, the question you and I must ask is; '*What are we going to do about what we hear?*' There are things that we can no longer ignore. Being part of the local church, knowing and experiencing the difficulties in getting young people to cross the threshold of a church building, Dad began to hang out in the places where the young people were.

Having read this newspaper article, he began to visit the local park. He would set off to see who was there, chatting with the guys and getting to know them. They were sitting around on the park benches just drinking to block out the cold and their surroundings.

All of a sudden, because of a headline, because of a decision from my dad, the youth in the park were no longer a stranger to him: they had become friends. God had given him such a love for them. Quite often my sister and I would waken on a Saturday morning and go into our living room to find these strangers sleeping off their drunken state from the night before! Some might think our parents were not cautious enough allowing such people in our home, but I can assure you that at least one of our parents was always with us; and do remember, God not only graces the called, but also the family that is called. So, I have quite vivid memories of sitting watching the cartoons in the morning with these guys sobering up around me, but never was I fazed by them at all!

This became a regular occurrence, so my dad tried reaching out to the church to see if they could facilitate these young people but they just didn't have the capacity and weren't sure what to do to help them.

Some of the locals didn't like the anti-social behaviour, as they thought these young people were bringing the community down. It was a difficult issue to deal with; but still my dad wanted to help turn things around. As he spent more time with the guys, he realised that a lot of the alcohol and drug abuse was occurring out of boredom. There was nothing to do in this small village, nowhere to go, so they just sat in the park and passed the time recreationally. After building relationships with them, he suggested opening a space in the village where they could come inside, out of the cold and play snooker, pool etc. This idea of shelter from the cold seemed to be well-received. At that time, there was a room available above the local chip shop, so we went along and looked at it to see if this would be suitable to take these young people off the streets.

After many nights in the park, many conversations and much prayer; on 5th November 1994, the doors of the youth centre were opened on the Main Street of Richhill. This provided a place in their community for the young people to go. They could come in and play games, socialise; and there was a small tuck shop as well. It was really successful with the young people leaving the park and coming to the centre instead. God was starting to work on the young people. One of the youths that Dad had befriended from the park, called Jason, was the first guy to get saved through the centre.

It was at that time my dad felt really inspired by the parable of the Good Samaritan in Luke 10. Essentially, this is what he was living out. He was taking the young people in from the streets and caring for them. God really spoke to him at this time and said to him about the Inn in the biblical account; that the people needed somewhere to recover and regain their strength. Therefore, he called the centre – *The Drop Inn*.

CHAPTER TWO

Taking a risk...

The vision was to have a continual presence in the community. To do this there was a need to have the centre open seven days a week. It wasn't long before Dad realised that this wasn't possible while working a full-time job. So he asked himself a question I still hear used to this day; *"What do we do? Do we opt for safety and comfort; or do we take a risk?"*

With the assurance that God had spoken, in birthing this desire within my dad to help these young people and with the success of the centre, he moved out in faith. Moving forward with the zeal for what God had called him to, he decided to leave his job. There were some difficult discussions at the time: friends who doubted this decision due to him having financial commitments and young children; and even those closest questioned him as to whether it was the *right* thing to do.

In her honesty, Mum says that even though she trusted Dad, she felt like she needed a word from God for her personally. One day as she was having her quiet time, she was reading the book of Haggai and she had a moment that would be significant for her when she read Haggai 2:19; *'Is there yet any seed left in the barn? Until now, the vine and the fig tree, the pomegranate and the olive tree have not borne fruit. 'From this day on I will bless you.'"*

In particular, the last part of that verse really spoke to her. A real sense of peace came upon her as she put her trust completely in God, knowing from that day onwards, He would bless them in their plans. So, despite having a mortgage, a wife and two young children, Dad resigned from his job. For several years, my dad had worked in furniture retail; but my parents believed that God would meet our financial needs. My dad brought us up to believe that whenever you are obedient to what God asks you to do, then blessing always follows.

The weekend that Drop Inn began turned out to be a more significant weekend than first thought. The doors opened for the first time on 5th November 1994. The following evening, while attending his son's Boys Brigade service, Les Brown (Jason's Dad) gave his life to Jesus, and, at the age of 47, committed the years he had remaining to serving the Lord. Jason had asked my dad to meet his father Les. Even though they lived in the same village, my parents had never met Les and his wife Carol Ann, but a few days later, they all sat together in their living room and a wonderful, fruitful partnership began.

The centre was open and it was filled with young people, with many deciding to follow Jesus. These were exciting days! A constant flow of young people would come in, and return, also bringing their friends: and so it continued. Pool tournaments were organised, plans were made to set up a football team. We were witnessing the early stages of seeing the dream becoming reality. Things were going really well until the week before Christmas, when my dad got a phone call from the landlord of the building. He told him that he had received complaints about what was going on, regarding the type of young people the centre was attracting. Because of this, we had to move out.

This was a huge blow! Dad had given up his job and, in some ways, had given up his reputation. Now it looked as if the adventure was coming to an abrupt end. Some suggested that we should set something up outside of the local area and bring young people to it. But we remained convinced that we were to be a continual presence in the community we wanted to see transformed, so we prayed and waited.

Shortly afterwards, the Indian restaurant on the Main Street in Richhill had just cleared out overnight. Right out of the blue, a three-storey building became available; and the same landlord phoned to say we could have all of the building or nothing! It was a little daunting, moving from a small room above a business to a three-storey building; but of course, the answer was: we would take it all! We moved in at the end of December 1994 and it became our home for just over five years, with an amazing group of people sharing their lives with the young people of Richhill.

Through time, we opened up a Sunday evening '*God Spot.*' This really spoke to those struggling with drugs and alcohol. And through this we were seeing amazing things happening from these gatherings and the *Drop Inn* centre. There were plans to expand the services even further; but unfortunately, just around that time, my granddad took ill. He was quite poorly, and all his commitments had to be cancelled. My dad had to help out a lot at that time. With the church to support him, however, thankfully at this time a team had started to gather around to allow the momentum to continue at the centre.

An unexpected change of direction...

January 1995 was another pivotal moment in the direction that God would take Drop Inn. My grandad, Joe, had a mission trip coming up to Belarus to help out with a soup kitchen charity in the capital Minsk; but with his ill health it just wasn't feasible for him to travel. Dad accepted the invitation on his behalf, and at the age of 33 had his first overseas mission experience. This was a trip that had a profound impact on him. Although he had seen situations of desperate need on TV news bulletins, this was the first time he came face to face with *real* poverty.

He also witnessed a spiritual hunger like he had never seen before. For seventy years, people were not allowed to attend a place of worship, so after all this time of communism, there was a spiritual vacuum within the country and so there was a great openness to share the Word of God. On one occasion after giving out little booklets containing the gospel of John on a public train in the city of Minsk, he turned back to see almost every passenger reading about *Jesus and how He came to dwell among us.* (John 1:14)

He visited the local hospitals and was shocked at the poor conditions. They didn't even have the most basic medical equipment. He witnessed poverty like he had never heard of before. While visiting one of the local hospitals, he met kids who were sick from the effects of the Chernobyl disaster just lying there with nothing to help them.

We all had watched the Chernobyl adverts on the TV; but he said it was even more impactful when you actually witness it for yourself. Many of you will relate to the emotions of such an experience. You may also relate to the feeling of knowing something needs to be done, but not sure what to do or where to begin. That is the feeling Dad came back from Belarus with. It was a trip that wasn't even meant for him; but it changed the course of his life and our family's life forever.

While Dad was away, people had been praying for Belarus and their hearts were moved when they heard the stories of kids in need of the most basic medical care, of families needing clothes on their backs and food on their tables. In the same way that a newspaper headline had confronted us with a need a few months previously, the real-life stories from Belarus confronted us too. What do we do? How do we respond?

When he returned back home, he spoke to the church leaders and others in the local area and told them about the awful conditions in Belarus. Everyone agreed that they would help. My granny, Florence, was quite instrumental in gathering all the supplies together. The aim was to send out aid to this community from which he had just returned. Everyone rallied around. Within just a matter of weeks, there were enough supplies to fill a container! It was hard work sorting everything as there were certain items we weren't allowed to ship, so all had to be planned very carefully; but the local community really stepped up and we were amazed at the response.

With the support of a community of people, we believed we could fill a lorry-load of food, clothes, medical supplies and gospel literature to bring to the neediest areas of Belarus. Les' brother donated his lorry for the trip. Friends, family, neighbours and churches donated the goods. On 10th July 1995, Dad, Les and Les' son Jason got into a 40-foot lorry and left Richhill to *'bring hope, help and healing to a hurting world.'*

Capital - Minsk

Major religion - Christianity

Official languages - Belarusian Russian

Population - 9,481,000

Currency - Belarusian ruble

Belarus formerly known as Byelorussia or White Russia, was the smallest of the three Slavic republics included in the Soviet Union, the larger two being Russia and Ukraine.

Belarus is a landlocked country bordered by Lithuania and Latvia to the north-west, by Russia to the north and east, by Ukraine to the south, and by Poland to the west. In area, it is roughly one-third the size of its southern neighbour, Ukraine.

The accident at the Chernobyl nuclear power plant in Ukraine in April 1986 resulted in a number of immediate and long-term consequences for the environment of Belarus, where most of the fallout occurred. In the early 21st century, about one-fifth of Belarus's land was still radioactively contaminated. In addition to the land damage, the medical and psychological costs of the accident included an increase in birth defects and cancer (particularly of the thyroid) and a declining birth rate, at least partly in response to fears of those defects. Environmental activists also have expressed concerns about poor air quality and pollution in Minsk and other major cities.

CHAPTER THREE

Stepping out into the unknown...

The first journey across Europe was once again stepping out into the unknown. Just like in the early days of setting up the centre, in making the first road trip to Belarus they found themselves not sure where the road was going to lead.... literally!

They were driving into territory they had never been before. The roads were bumpy, the journey was difficult and the road signs didn't make any sense! That was all before having to navigate the border crossings! Poland was not part of the European Union then so they had to use papers to get from Germany into Poland, then more papers to get from Poland into Belarus. It was not an easy situation but they made it! After three days in an 8x7-foot cabin they were greeted at the delivery site in Minsk, the capital city of Belarus, with a lorry full of aid.

This was a memorable trip in so many ways. It was the fulfilment of months of preparation and an expression of love from a local community. This was only six months after Les had given the rest of his life to following Jesus. Now he found himself not only travelling across Europe, but telling his story in prisons and public parks in the city of Minsk.

In Richhill, we were asking questions about what should be done with the goods that didn't meet the criteria of humanitarian aid. There were so many donations of things that couldn't be used, so my granny opened a little corner shop in the square of the village. It was only open for a few hours on a Thursday afternoon and a Saturday morning but she started to sell some things. The sales kept increasing so we also went to the cash-and-carry to expand the range of products. My granny, at age 58, was becoming an entrepreneur. What else could happen?

She sold chocolate bars and *anything at all* really just to raise funds for further trips to Belarus. (Sometimes I wonder was it my parents that invented the pop-up shop? It was certainly the first one in our area!) She was determined to do her part; and even with the limited time it was open, she was able to generate enough money to pay for the container, the cost of diesel and shipping. It was a real family effort! Then it snowballed.

News started to spread about our efforts throughout the local area. People started to appear from far and wide with donations for Belarus. My granny would take the items into her shop and box them. She must have nearly boxed the entire first and second container all by herself! Without a doubt, she was setting a high bar for us to follow! The second container was ready to go by October 1995.

As the donations grew, my dad decided to take on a retail shop in Richhill that was open all week; and there the first Drop Inn charity shop was established. This was the first and only charity shop in the area at that time.

We quickly realised that it was working well; but if we wanted to send more containers then we needed more stock. The decision was made to expand and open two further shops in neighbouring towns, Markethill and Tandragee, located six miles on either side of Richhill. This allowed us to always be connected with people in each area knowing us, and also reduced the travel between shops to a minimum, keeping overhead costs down.

I could see God had clearly burdened my dad for this ministry. He continued to grow the work and drive the containers each time to and from Belarus. These were long and arduous journeys.

There were no comforts back then on the lorry. Their bed for the one week of travelling each time was a small mattress in the cabin of the lorry. They would take turns, one driving through the night while the other slept. Their food for the week was whatever snacks they could squeeze into a cool-box. I still don't understand it, but corned beef was a firm favourite! Their communication back home was limited until they reached their destination and their showering facilities for the journey were minimal, so as you can imagine, the lorry needed to be well aired-out by the time it made its way home!

For Dad leaving his young family and his wife behind was also sacrificial. My mum really missed him when he was away; it was difficult for her as she was still grieving the loss of her own precious dad, Cecil, who passed away suddenly the previous year. My grandad had been outside in the garden cutting the grass; and when he didn't come in, my granny went to see where he was. She found him in the garage having suffered a massive heart attack.

His life and testimony had made an impact on so many people; and his passing was a great loss to us and so many who knew him. Cecil was a passionate man who loved Jesus: Mum recalls him on his knees in prayer every night. This was the first-time death had touched our family so closely.

Knowing that there was now a void that could not be filled, the challenge, for my mum in particular, was how to continue the legacy of faithfully following Jesus. She pondered how the next generation could see more, how she could build on the momentum gathered by those we follow after. With the growing need in the local community and the experience of loss in the family, God began to bring life to the embryonic vision he had given to my parents.

Lost in translation…

Around this time when he was driving the containers, Les soon became established as my dad's official driving buddy, helping share the burden of the long trek to Belarus. As it was before the invention of Google Maps, mobile phones etc., they were navigating new roads. In addition to that, I am unsure even if they thought about the language barriers as they travelled through different countries: they would have joked; *"Here comes Dumb and Dumber,"* yet they never could quite figure out which was which!

The roads were now slightly familiar, but there was nothing familiar about an Eastern European winter. Road conditions were poor; when they reached the Polish border they had to wait for 14 hours before getting through. Being unable to call home, border crossings became the place that intensified feelings of discouragement in the cold, dark hours of the night.

On their fifth visit, Dad and Les sat 24 hours at the border to take another lorry load of supplies into Belarus. It was minus 20 degrees Celsius, the night heater wouldn't work and every food item they had brought with them was frozen including the treasured bottles of Coke. For the first time they thought to themselves; *'This is too uncomfortable, it's too difficult, I can't do it again.'*

They felt that they needed a word from the Lord. The host family that my dad was staying with the following night felt God had spoken to them about his arriving. They shared what God had laid on their hearts, which was Galatians 6:9; *'Let us not become weary in doing good, for at the proper time we will reap a harvest if we do not give up.'* In the most difficult moment, the darkest of night was

25

the place they learned the most significant lesson. At their lowest point, God spoke. When they were at their most vulnerable, the Holy Spirit gave courage to persevere.

As you will see, as you continue to read, their story goes on; but Dad will often reflect back to that night at the border and remark on what we would have missed out on if he had given up. Building for the generation coming after us would have been missed if things stopped at that time. That journey became another turning point as he now knew he had to continue with the work that he felt the Lord had asked him to do. The Scripture shared by the host family on that trip, from then on became like a mantra for him.

As challenging as many of the trips were, by the time they came home there was still such an excitement about what was happening in the relationships that were being built. I always enjoyed hearing stories when something was lost in translation. On those early trips, finding the storage facility for the lorry was difficult due to the road signs, so they rang for directions. One time, the local contact who spoke English answered the phone and asked Dad; "Where are you?" They looked for the nearest sign and said they were on "Siton Street." After taking a few moments to compose himself from laughing the translator said; "It would take a long time to find you as 'Siton' is the word for 'stop;' you are looking at a stop-sign!"

It's only now when I look back, I never realised how hard my parents worked away from the unseen eye. Dad would be sorting accounts, maintaining the lorry, delivering stock to and from the shops and then to the buyers. And then, there's my mum. On those early trips before leaving home, my mum would have planned out the journey in terms of how much food Dad and Les would need, and she would have started to cook and bake, freezing where possible. She would also pack the cooler with tins of stew, corned beef and plenty of sweets.

It was a few years later they were delighted to see the smiling face of Colonel Sanders, as KFC began to pop up across Eastern Europe. On one occasion in Poland, after ordering his chicken by pointing at the screen, Les was asked a question in Polish he didn't understand. Convinced she was asking him did he want spicy or regular, Les responded more slowly and loudly each time she asked. He said, *"R-E-G-U-L-A-R."* Finally a local who spoke English put them both out of their misery by telling Les; *"She is asking: Do you want to sit in or takeaway?"*

Even with the language barriers, relationships were deepening with those who were faithfully serving their churches and communities. It is worth highlighting the importance of Drop Inn's first long-term mission partner in Belarus, Leonid Biruk. His wife Olga and family are still friends of Drop Inn and were key in the developing of projects and partnerships right across the nation. Leonid recently wrote to me and said; *"The first time I met Ronnie was in March 1997. At that time I was in charge of international relations in our denomination, then called 'Union of Christians of Evangelical Faith' in Belarus. The circle of my responsibilities was large and included dealing with humanitarian aid.*

"That morning I had received a phone call from Lilia Shapchits, who worked for a Messianic Fellowship in Minsk, requesting my assistance in a very serious case relating to humanitarian aid from Ireland. 'You are our last hope,' she said. It was a time when there was

mad cow disease in the United Kingdom and the Belarus government had just introduced some very strict customs restrictions. To make the story short, I was able to solve that problem. Immediately Ronnie invited me and my wife Olga to Ireland and in May 1997 we went to Northern Ireland.

"We fell in love with Northern Ireland and with the Irish people, especially with Ronnie and his family. It was the beginning of a great friendship which I value so much. For the last 22 years, it has involved hundreds of people both from Belarus, United Kingdom, Ireland and dozens of other countries. Ronnie and other guys were coming sometimes up to five times a year to Belarus: they were bringing humanitarian aid twice a year, then bringing teams twice a year and once a year, with a group of young people for a youth camp in Belarus."

Location - Ukraine

Dates - April 26, 1986 – May 4, 1986

Chernobyl disaster, accident in 1986 at the Chernobyl nuclear power station in the Soviet Union. It was the worst disaster in the history of nuclear power generation. The Chernobyl power station was situated at the settlement of Pryp'yat, 10 miles (16 km) north-west of the city of Chernobyl (Ukrainian: Chornobyl) and 65 miles (104 km) north of Kiev, Ukraine. The station consisted of four reactors, each capable of producing 1,000 megawatts of electric power. It had come online in 1977–83.

29

The disaster occurred on April 25–26, 1986, when technicians at reactor Unit 4 attempted a poorly designed experiment. Workers shut down the reactor's power-regulating system and its emergency safety systems, and they withdrew most of the control rods from its core while allowing the reactor to continue running at seven per cent power. These mistakes were compounded by others, and at 1:23 AM on April 26 the chain reaction in the core went out of control. Several explosions triggered a large fireball and blew off the heavy steel and concrete lid of the reactor. This and the ensuing fire in the graphite reactor core released large amounts of radioactive material into the atmosphere, where it was carried great distances by air currents. A partial meltdown of the core also occurred.

CHAPTER FOUR

The effects of Chernobyl...

After a few years of delivering humanitarian aid, we began to ask if there was anything more that we could do for the children we had met in the different hospitals. Many of the children in the hospital were there as a result of the Chernobyl disaster of April 1986, a horrendous nuclear accident that cost many lives. The consequences were still being felt a decade later. It's hard for the rest of the world to imagine the devastation this disaster has visited on the people, the children and the land. Because of the unprecedented scale of the accident, even scientists and subject experts can't predict what the future holds for those who live in the shadow of Chernobyl.

On April 26, 1986, at 1:23 a.m., an explosion and fire occurred in Reactor number four of the Chernobyl nuclear power plant in what is now Ukraine. Before engineers and scientists could get it under control, 190 tons of highly radioactive material were released into the atmosphere. The radioactive particles rained down not only on Chernobyl, but all over Ukraine, as well as the neighbouring countries of Belarus and Russia, and drifted over to other European countries such as Poland. Scientists estimate that the amount of particles released was equivalent to the effect of 20 nuclear bombs.

The Chernobyl accident remains the largest peacetime nuclear disaster ever. Its effects would linger for years to come.

When we were told by the medics that a holiday to Northern Ireland would improve the children's health and boost their immune system, plans were soon put in place. In 1996, we started an initiative to bring some of the children who were affected by Chernobyl to Northern Ireland. We gathered children from the local orphanages and hospitals and brought them across to spend three weeks with families in the local area who were willing to open their homes and love these children.

People in our community had sent their donations, now we were asking would they open their homes to receive. Not only did they open their homes; but they opened their hearts, and they loved and blessed these children in such a tangible way. A three-week holiday included trips to the beach, to the zoo, fun days sponsored by local community groups, visits to the Mayor's office in different towns; and much, much more. Over a ten-year period, we hosted more than 250 children. We love hearing stories of families who have kept in touch with those children, many of whom are now adults, to this day.

We continued sending containers and bringing the Chernobyl children over for holidays. I would like to introduce you to one of the children who came on the Chernobyl children's programme, Irina...

Irina was a young girl who had been left abandoned by her parents, rejected because of her physical appearance, unfortunately not an unusual story. Irina was born with cleft lip and palate. As a result, she was very shy, reserved and sad. In 1997, Irina came to Northern Ireland and stayed with a local lady, Evelyn Robinson, and her family in Middletown, Co Armagh. During the holiday, Irina was brought to the Royal Hospital in Belfast. They said it was the worst case they had ever seen. After consultation, one of the top surgeons offered his services free of charge to perform the operation to repair her cleft lip and palate.

Irina's operation was a success. It was so amazing to watch this little girl's face light up when she smiled for the first time. As with all the kids who visited, it was always hard to say goodbye, but Irina was able to return to the orphanage with a greater sense of dignity and worth. Today, Irina is 24-years-old, living in her own apartment in the Brest region of Belarus. She is working as a cleaner and sometimes attends the local Baptist church.

One of the parts of the Bible that has been an anchor-point for Drop Inn since the beginning is in Matthew 25. Jesus speaking: '*I was hungry and you fed me, I was thirsty and you gave me a drink, I was a stranger and you invited me into your home, naked and you gave me clothing, sick and you cared for me, in prison and you visited me.*' The people were confused and asked Jesus, '*Lord, when did we do all that?*' Jesus, as He so often does, gives this stunning response: '*When you did it to ONE OF THE LEAST of these, you were doing it to me.*' God has chosen to make His presence, His kindness, His love known through ordinary people like us, like you.

A pastor's son…

One of the children from the first group that came to visit in 1997 was a young boy called Anatoliy Oliferchik. He stayed in the home of Richhill couple Paul and Patricia Andrews. In Belarus, his dad,

Nikolai was a pastor of a church in Beryoza, their home city. A few months before Anatoliy came to Northern Ireland, Nikolai had to get some temporary work outside of the country in Moscow, such was the pressure to care for his family and the church. At the end of his three-week holiday, Anatoliy went back home to Belarus with two full suitcases for his whole family that Paul and Patricia had filled. Nikolai was overwhelmed and sent a letter expressing the depth of his gratitude, how God had used this couple to meet their needs.

As letters continued to go back and forth between Richhill and Beryoza, Paul and Patricia asked my dad a question that would ultimately add an extra dimension to the ministry of Drop Inn: *"Is there any way to support this pastor financially?"*

Once again, the answer was 'yes!' Through this incident, a pastoral support element was birthed. Today we are able to support and cheer on the work of 78 pastors in 61 different cities around the world. I will share the stories of a few others as we go on.

Right from the beginning, we were passionate about involving as many people as possible in as many different ways as possible. Some had got involved through donating goods or opening their homes. Then we extended the invitation for those who wanted to see and experience the various projects for themselves. We began taking groups to visit the orphanages and hospitals in the cities where we had been supporting. People were impacted by these trips in a way that just hearing the stories could never do. This is something we continue to prioritise to this day, to the point where we have taken over 1,000 people on various mission experiences into many countries. I will tell the stories of some of those who have travelled in the following chapters.

CHAPTER FIVE

Developing character...

When I was thirteen, I had the opportunity to go in the lorry with my dad and visit Belarus. I thought this was so cool: much better than being at school! It was a real adventure going away. I loved sitting on the cabin bed in the lorry following the map as we journeyed across France, into Germany, then through Poland and crossing the border into Belarus. It was really significant that I got to witness the impact Drop Inn were having in this part of the world at a young age. At the time I didn't think it impacted me much but clearly, looking back now, it was one of the environments that has moulded me into the person I am today.

On a trip to the church in Belarus, we met a singing group. My dad thought this would be a good opportunity to raise further awareness of the help needed in the country by bringing them over on a tour to Northern Ireland and the mainland. The singing group travelled from Kalinkovichi, a town in the south-eastern part of Belarus. Vasia played the keyboard and was accompanied by Tanya S, Tanya M, Elena, Ira, Luda and Elena B. They sang gospel songs in their own language and wore traditional Belarusian dresses. We brought them to Northern Ireland; the tour then travelled through different areas and raised the profile of the Belarus people.

This was a huge sacrifice for my family as it was an eight-week tour throughout the United Kingdom. Dad was away on the road; Mum was at home with me and my sister. There were a lot of sacrifices made so that the people of Belarus could get the help they so desperately needed.

Building for the future…

During this time I was still at school, studying at Portadown College. I enjoyed school, especially the rugby, and had the opportunity to be on the first rugby team. Actually, I later realised that in my first 2 years at Portadown College, unbeknown to me, sitting in my French class was my future wife Judith! Not noticing her is something she still reminds me of to this day!

My relationship with Judith began at the start of our final year in Portadown College. She had signed up for one of the mission trips we were running to Belarus and Ukraine and it was there we actually met properly. It wasn't long before I knew I wanted to spend the rest of my life with her. She always brought out the best in me. I'm a better father, friend and follower of Jesus because she continues to do that, even to this day.

When I turned eighteen, I decided to take a year out to help my dad instead of going to university. I helped in the charity shops and by loading the containers for Belarus three to four times that year; and just loved supporting the thriving communities there. This just developed the drive and ambition I had deep within me to help others. As a result of this, I didn't return to my education.

I got on board with the work full-time, especially working with the youth. I loved helping young people.

My becoming involved in youth work felt like the most natural thing for me to do. I had been around the environment of the youth centre since I was ten and saw the difference that being loved and supported had on teenagers. Even in our home life, Mum and Dad were foster-carers, and again, I saw the difference it made when young people were shown their true worth. Over the years, as my role changed, the work among the young people continued to flourish under the leadership of Ian Liggett. Ian has an amazing story of finding and following Jesus, but we'd need another book to tell it!

At our core has always been prioritising relationships, so even at times over the years when we haven't had a building to meet in, communication with local young people remained open. Now Ian is still meeting up with the young men and women who came through our youth centres from years past; they are into their twenties, with their own families.

My mum is a woman of prayer. From the day I was born, she would pray regularly for the right woman to be my wife. She was very excited to meet Judith and felt this was the woman she had been praying for. We got engaged when we were both nineteen; two years later, on 31st August 2006, we entered into this beautiful covenant of marriage. We stood before God declaring that we were going to love and honour each other, celebrate the good, work hard through the difficult times and pursue the call God had on our lives together.

We were both very aligned in our ambitions for the Kingdom of God and had a real desire to help others. In the early years of our married life, we had the joy of travelling into different Drop Inn projects around the world. In January 2009, we had our first child, Caleb, who by April of that same year became Drop Inn's youngest missionary. (a record he still holds today!) He first came with us on the team we were leading to Venezuela. I'm not sure he remembers too much of his first mission experience but we loved introducing him to all the kids and families we were working with around Barquisimeto.

Knowing the impact of experiencing another culture and a completely different way of life at a young age, we decided to bring our kids to visit the school projects in Burkina Faso when we felt they were ready. To date, Caleb has been on a team visit with Judith, they went in 2017 and our second child, Eli came with me in January 2019. Both of them had an incredible time; we can't wait to bring our girls in the future too.

Empowering locals...

We supported local people so they could equip and empower their communities. Through the church in Belarus we were able to build relationships with people in Ukraine, and we started sending supplies there also. This then spread to Albania, where we came alongside those that were pastoring in the local area. These were all first-generation Believers and pastors, something which I thought was fascinating, as I am a fifth-generation Believer! Albania was a difficult country for these young pastors; as you flew into the country, at the airport when you arrived, there were signs up saying; 'There is no God in Albania!' That was just the level of communism in that area.

In year 2000, Dad was put in contact with a man in Albania called Valter Xhelili. Valter was pastoring a church in Fier, a city of 200,000 people in the south-west of the country. There had been a civil war in 1997 and many of the church members had fled, so he restarted the work with very few people. He married Arta in 1998. They were both involved in what was truly pioneering work. They had lived in the grip of communism for years, where it was forbidden to believe in God, so not only were they first generation Believers, they were first generation pastors.

Drop Inn have been financially supporting Valter and Arta since they met in Tirana airport back in the year 2000. We have supported their projects in helping people in need; there are many families that need help. In my conversation with Valter, he stressed that the support from Drop Inn has been so much more than financial. He credits Drop Inn with playing the main role in the life of his ministry and in his own personal life too. He is grateful for the mentors that Mum and Dad have been to him and his wife. As Valter summed up his relationship with Drop Inn, he used this beautiful line; "*We were trusted.*"

I can't help but think that's what true partnership looks like. In Apostle Paul's letter to the Philippians, he thanks God as he remembers them in prayer; '*because of their partnership in the gospel from the first day until now,*' Philippians 1:5 NIV. In our relationship with local people on the front lines of community engagement, seeking Gospel transformation, we want our partnership to communicate this: **we** believe in **you**, **we** believe in what **you** are doing, it is **our** joy to stand alongside **you**, **we** trust **you**.

Not long after meeting Valter and Arta, we had the privilege of connecting with Akil and Lindita Pano in Tirana. These were Lindita's words; *"We remember the first time we met Ronnie and Neville at the airport in Tirana in 2001. Since then it has been an amazing partnership in the journey we have walked together. We were back from our five-year mission in Shkodra and were still struggling to start GOC (Gospel of Christ church) in Tirana. We will never forget how Drop Inn came alongside and helped. We were really poor and didn't have any resources except a vision and a calling from God.*

"Ronnie and Carolyn have been amazing with sending humanitarian aid over for a long time. We started with the first summer camps in 2002 and Drop Inn were the visitors and sponsors for that camp.

"We still keep doing that camp as it is a great tool of discipleship and growth. We still remember the teams from Northern Ireland travelling by old buses to arrive in Albania and be with us in the summer camp. The other teams that were coming to help us with evangelism were sleeping on our kitchen floor while the winters were so cold and we had power cuts all the time. Drop Inn have helped with rent support, pastoral support, summer camps, humanitarian aid, teams and support for the poorest of the poor.

"Ronnie and Carolyn have not only been amazing supporters of GOC but amazing friends that we can share our hearts and burdens. Today GOC is established and one of the biggest churches in the country and is involved in church planting work in Albania and beyond.

"Drop Inn remains our faithful partner in this call of God for this nation. You have a major part of what God had done in our midst and this ministry."

I'm convinced that's what true partnership looks like: standing with people to see their vision come to life. You can imagine the joy we experience when we see how God's hand has been on the Pano family and their church, how God has graced them to establish an incredible Kingdom work in the capital city of Albania, and their carrying that across the Balkan nations. God has truly raised them up, *'for a time such as this.'*

Capital - Tirana
Major religion - None
Official languages - Albanian
Population - 2,886,026
Currency - Lek (L)

Albania a country in southern Europe, located in the western part of the Balkan Peninsula on the Strait of Otranto, the southern entrance to the Adriatic Sea. The capital city is Tirana.

Because of its location on the Adriatic and Ionian seas, Albania has long served as a bridgehead for various nations and empires seeking conquest abroad. In the 2nd century BCE the Illyrians were conquered by the Romans, and from the end of the 4th century CE they were ruled by the Byzantine Empire. After suffering centuries of invasion by Visigoths, Huns, Bulgars, and Slavs, the Albanians were finally conquered by the Ottoman Turks in the 15th century.

Albania was declared independent in 1912, but the following year the demarcation of its boundaries by the great powers of Europe (Austria-Hungary, Britain, France, Germany, Italy, and Russia) assigned about half its territory and people to neighbouring states. Ruled as a monarchy between the World Wars, Albania emerged from the violence of World War II as a communist state that fiercely protected its sovereignty and in which almost all aspects of life were controlled by the ruling party. But with the collapse of other communist regimes beginning in 1989, new social forces and democratic political parties emerged in Albania. That shift reflected the country's continuing orientation toward the West, and it accorded with the Albanian people's long-standing appreciation of Western technology and cultural achievements; even while retaining their own ethnic identity, cultural heritage, and individuality.

CHAPTER SIX

The shoebox appeal...

We widened the prospect of involvement when we began our annual Christmas shoebox appeal. We were so grateful for the school groups, Boys and Girls Brigades, among others, who each Christmas would fill a shoebox of gifts, so that we could give the children in Belarus the only present most of them would receive all year. To witness the faces of young boys and girls light up as they took each item out of their box is a beautiful thing. To be able to hand a child, who had been abandoned as a little baby, a gift from another part of the world and not only tell them they are valued and loved but to show them practically, is a moving experience.

The Drop Inn Shoebox Appeal runs each year to provide a little bit of joy and happiness to children of all ages. It was a progression from the earlier days when Drop Inn would send lorries full of supplies to Belarus. It's a fairly simple concept where we ask people to wrap a shoebox in Christmas paper and then fill it up. We use what we call the four **W**'s to help people with ideas. These are:

1. **W**ash: items such as soap, toothpaste, toothbrush, face cloth, sponge etc.
2. **W**rite: pens, pencils, notebooks and other stationary.

3. **W**ear: hats, gloves, scarves, T-shirts.
4. **WOW**: this is the fun thing which can be a toy, games, a teddy bear, sweets. We encourage people to be imaginative in making the gift extra special!

These boxes are taken into one of our shops or drop-off locations. We bring them to be sorted at our headquarters. Each box has to be checked before they can go through customs.

In 2016 we began a partnership with Team Hope, who are based in Ireland. They are able to send shoeboxes to countries across Eastern Europe and parts of Africa: which means we can now send shoeboxes into even more countries. In 2018 in total we distributed 259,079 shoeboxes, meaning 259,079 children received a gift last Christmas, many of whose families have to survive in very difficult conditions. This is something we continue to devote much of our attention to at the end of each year.

For all these projects to develop in the way they have, it required more funds to be raised back in Northern Ireland. Les and Carol Ann took on the responsibility of developing our charity shop model, which continues to be our biggest source of revenue for what we are involved in across the world.

Much of the success of the past 25 years is due to our hard-working staff taking responsibility for stock, volunteers and customer care in our shops scattered across Northern Ireland and beyond. Our shops rely on the donations of the people in each community. It is their generosity that continues to sustain so much of what we do around the world. There is a huge variety of goods available: clothes, bric-a-brac, books, furniture and much more. As it is vital to each shop to keep on replenishing their stock, we have vans out on the road every day, collecting and delivering items in homes all over the country. Between our shop staff, office staff, van drivers, volunteers and the public, they all play their part in sending *hope* to some of the most difficult places across the world.

CHAPTER SEVEN

Developing out of relationship, not business...

God had taught my dad that Kingdom is about relationship. With that being instilled into him, this would determine that when we looked for a shop in a new area, it was usually on the basis of a relationship with someone local who had a heart for the work we were doing. Then it was important to find the best, most accessible location possible. We had done that in Richhill and Markethill and most definitely in Tandragee with Lorna Boyce, who is still on the Main Street all these years later, and continues to be an important part of the Drop Inn family. It wasn't too long after that, when we made our way north to Larne.

Heather Kennedy had been introduced to Drop Inn a couple of years previous as part of her diploma she was doing in Belfast Bible College. She volunteered one day a week in our charity shops, then travelled on one of our group trips to Belarus. She was also a great help in our Chernobyl children's programme, volunteering her time and organising many of the fun days for the kids. In response to what she had seen and experienced, Heather asked; *"Could I do a shop?"* The shop had been opened a few months and a lady called

Martha Steenson came in to volunteer. We are so glad she did, because when Heather moved on, Martha took over the running of the shop and is still there today, continuing to be a wonderful ambassador for our charity in Larne.

You also need to know about one of our customers in Larne, an unsung hero, Amelia Johnston. Since we opened our shop in Larne, she began to make shoeboxes for the Christmas appeal. She would begin to pack them in April and by the time it got to the deadline in November she had filled hundreds! One year she filled over 900 shoeboxes for us to bring to the neediest kids in Eastern Europe. We estimate she has filled around 10,000 shoeboxes on her own; and much at her own expense.

Location, location, location…

We went slightly 'off script' when we made our way to Carrickfergus. We didn't know many people in the area; but we had been told about a lady called Joan. Joan had been working in St Vincent de Paul's charity shop after the death of her husband, and had recently retired from her position. After praying with close friends, they had a beautiful moment of clarity: from that time, Joan agreed to lead the work in Carrickfergus, if we could find a shop. As Les walked through the streets of Carrickfergus looking for a prime location, he found himself down a side street, looking at an empty, unimpressive building. Of course, for every new shop, Les always prayed that we would find the best location; but this was the first time he had such a strong impression that this was the right place.

I love how God gets our attention. In the moments where we could ignore or walk away, He reveals something we can't see in the natural. So we opened our next shop on this little street, off the beaten track, with a lady we were just getting to know.

We are so grateful for Joan and the team she has gathered around her. We love the testimony of these ladies within the local community and we are amazed at what God has done through them. They could tell story after story of how prayers have been answered, people have found comfort and experienced healing. Joan tells the story of a baby girl, born to one of the customers they had got to know in the shop. They were told the baby wouldn't survive very long, so the baby's granny brought her in and the ladies began to pray and continued to pray. This little girl is now three-years-old and is doing really well. It's a place of constant prayer. It's a place that still goes 'off script;' but isn't that so often the places where Jesus shows up in the most incredible ways!

Widening the nets...

As the retail stores continued to expand, so did our connections throughout the world. With more shops opening and more communities supporting us, we were able not only to maintain the commitments that were made but to establish new relationships beyond the borders of Belarus. The first place we went was Rivne Bible Seminary in the west of Ukraine. Through a mutual friend, we were introduced to the director of the Bible seminary, Paul Vaselyts, and began to fill containers of humanitarian aid to distribute to the neediest areas across Ukraine through their ministry.

When students graduate, they are sent to a village with very few Christians and little Christian influence, areas of spiritual and physical poverty. As they adapt to the life of the place they are sent, and build relationships with local people, they begin to plant churches. They currently have mission stations in 21 villages across Ukraine and it's into these places that we bring gifts of love and hope. When I think of what our friends are doing in the Ukraine, I am reminded of Luke 10, where followers of Jesus are sent ahead in pairs to the towns and places Jesus planned to visit. As they adapted and were welcomed, they were then to announce; *'the kingdom of God is near you now.'* Luke 10:9.

A good friendship also developed with another mission organisation in Ukraine called *Morning Star,* based in Rivne. We have sent humanitarian aid throughout the years. They were recipients of our Christmas shoebox appeal which helped further the work they were involved in locally. We brought many young people to run camps for teens and twenties who came from many parts of Europe. In 2005 they undertook the restoration of a collapsed camp for children. This was a massive building which required a lot of work. We were able to provide the funds and materials to see this camp facility brought back to life. Les led many work teams to assist in this big restoration project. Some of the photos we have from these trips, especially of the guys painting high walls, would give our local health and safety officers nightmares!

Since the completion of the project, the first programme to run from the building was for orphaned children in the Rokito region. There are 40 children who have been receiving help every month from Drop Inn ever since. In 2010, a camp was opened on the site for disabled young people. From May to September every year, young people can come on a ten-day holiday with finances coming from Drop Inn. The director of the charity is Gregoriy Khomich, who in spite of the language barrier can share the many happy memories that he and the children continue to hold closely. He closed out his messages to me saying; *"Blessings to Ronnie and Carolyn and Drop Inn family in your immensely great cause for the Lord!"*

In 2007, Alex Tretyak was appointed director of the Bible seminary. We have enjoyed a great partnership with him. When taking on the role from Paul as director, Paul wanted Drop Inn to be the first people Alex was introduced to, saying we were the *'most long-term faithful partners'* they had. Alex came to Drop Inn's European conference in 2008 and met my parents. He says, respectfully, that he was shocked by the simplicity of a couple with such a big responsibility. He was amazed that they immediately felt *like* parents, as if he had known them his whole life. In my conversations with many Drop Inn partners this father/mother language became common when speaking of their relationship with Mum and Dad.

The idea of family has been at the centre of everything Drop Inn has done; more than anything else, that's what true partnership looks like. We want people to know we are not just going to pray for them or give to what they are doing but they are part of family. We continued to offer different opportunities to come and meet the Drop Inn family, to see what God was doing in another part of the world and encourage one another in the process. For many years the annual highlight became our summer youth trips, when young people from all over Northern Ireland would come together to travel to Belarus, Ukraine or Albania, sometimes all three on the one trip.

For many of the young people that joined us on our summer adventures, it was their first mission trip, their first experience of another culture. On the 28th July 2000, twelve young people arrived in Minsk, Belarus to be part of a multi-national youth camp. It became practice to spend the first couple of days, split up into different host families throughout the city, experiencing different foods, homes and customs.

We spent one week on a little island surrounded by the river Neman outside of Minsk. There was no running water or electricity and our only access to the island was small dinghy boats but we loved it even though it was outside our comfort zone. Our days were filled with sports activities and our evenings with music, two of the most effective ways of breaking down language barriers. The following summer we returned to this special little island, with more young people than before: young people who had decided to give up their summer holidays and their most basic home comforts to be stretched and challenged in their faith journey.

A great friend to this day, Stuart Argue, had this to say about his experiences on these summer trips; *"I can truly say the Drop Inn summer trips impacted me and shaped the course of my life. I had the privilege of going on seven five-week mission summer teams right across Eastern Europe. It was on these trips that I learned what it was to have real faith in God, grow in passion for Jesus and see the great needs across Europe, develop gifting and also make decisions as to how I would live in the future. A very special personal moment for me was my water baptism in Albania on my first ever team. I often kept journals on these trips: here is a snippet from 6th August 2003, the first time I had been asked to testify publicly on the streets..."*

Location: Slovakia. *We are getting ready to go out and evangelise tonight...was told 30 minutes beforehand I was doing my testimony on the streets... Woohoo! Some man got saved tonight at the evangelism, it was brilliant and I think one was saved last night....*

"I always went on these teams to serve and tell people about the love and saving power of Jesus, but in turn it was me who ended up being blessed beyond belief! I have so, so many memories and miraculous moments that I often recall from these God adventures. God continually showed up as we stepped out in faith, I would love to be doing it all over again."

Tough times...

In 2001, my grandad Joe passed away. He had been ill for such a long time, yet through his suffering he remained firm in his faith and was passionate about Jesus. His death was deeply upsetting but it was also a *wake-up moment* for me. I had spent my teenage years struggling to hold on to my faith. Now it felt like I was either going to have to decide to follow Jesus in the way my granddad had demonstrated, or not at all. The days of sitting on the fence for me were over. It had to be all or nothing! Even though I continue to mess up, I think from that moment I've really wanted to be *'all in.'*

Grandad's death also meant transition for my family in terms of our church life. We decided to leave Richhill Elim. My parents and my sister settled in a church outside Armagh and I joined Emmanuel church in Lurgan.

Years previously, Dad felt God had given him a vision to plant a church in our local area. In the spring of 2005, my parents had just come home from their latest overseas mission trip. It was a Saturday. When they walked through the front door to the usual mountain of post, amongst all the letters was an envelope and inside it was the single biggest donation Drop Inn had received up to that point. It was for £6,000, with a note saying it was to be used for whatever was the most pressing need at the time. All the projects were up to date with their financial support, so what was it for?

The following Monday, Les had already planned to visit a site which held portable buildings, to see if there was anything suitable that could be used for a church. He found an old school building: a chemistry classroom, to be exact; that would be a perfect fit for the space we had hoped to set something on. Les knew nothing about the cheque when he phoned Dad telling him he had good news and bad news. The good news was that they would sell us the building for £1,000 but the bad news was that the cost to take it apart, transport it and to reassemble was going to cost £5,000. Total cost = £6,000!

This didn't feel like bad news to Dad, he was so excited! It felt like an amazing confirmation of walking in the plan of God. It certainly assured us that now was the right time to implement the vision. Two days in advance of finding the building, God had provided the finances needed to plant a church.

When the building arrived on site, it was a team effort to transform a chemistry classroom into a space for Sunday gatherings. Walls came down, new flooring was laid and an unused space was given new life: just what we wanted to see happening in the lives of those we would soon be engaging with. Drop Inn Community Church had its first Sunday morning service on 4th September 2005. The desire was for people to experience the Abundant Life Jesus said He came to bring.

Our vision was to reach the unchurched youth and people who had become disillusioned with formal religion. Our desire was to see such people coming into relationship with Jesus, becoming members of the church, developing in maturity, being equipped for ministry and fulfilling their purpose in God's Kingdom. The church gave us a great base to train and equip others to go on mission and to pray together for the expansion and growth of vision.

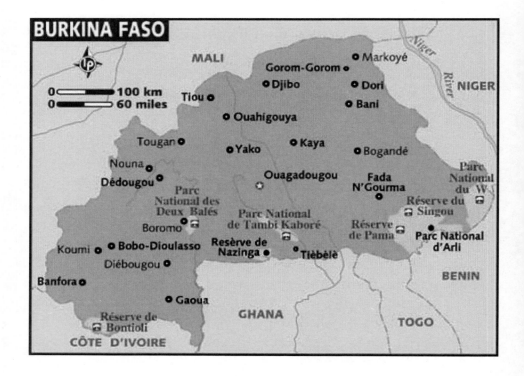

Capital - Ouagadougou
Major religion Islam
Official Language - French
Population - 17,322,796
Currency - CFA Franc

Burkina Faso is one of the poorest countries in Africa:
a landlocked country with little going in or out. A former
French colony, it gained independence as Upper Volta
in 1960. The name Burkina Faso, which means "Land of
Incorruptible People," was adopted in 1984. The capital,
Ouagadougou, is in the centre of the country and lies about
500 miles (800 km) from the Atlantic Ocean. As a result of

the extreme poverty and poor prospects, AIDS has become a major problem.

The climate of Burkina Faso is generally sunny, hot, and dry. Two principal climate zones can be distinguished. The Sahelian zone in the north is semiarid steppe, characterized by three to five months of rainfall, which is often erratic. To the south, in the Sudanic zone, the climate becomes increasingly of the tropical wet-dry type, with a greater variability of temperature and rainfall and greater total rainfall than the north.

More than half the population is Muslim. About one-fifth of the Burkinabé are Roman Catholic, and one-sixth follow traditional religions. Most of the remainder are Protestant or non-religious. The seat of the Roman Catholic archbishopric is in Ouagadougou, and there are several bishoprics throughout the country.

CHAPTER EIGHT

Connecting the dots...

The first project we developed outside of Europe was in Burkina Faso in West Africa. To tell this story, I need to go back to 1978 to show how the dots connect to reveal a wonderful picture that God is still shaping.

A young man, Etienne Yameogo, left his home city of Koudougou in Africa to attend the International Bible Training Institute in England, here in the United Kingdom. This was a big step of faith for Etienne, moving across the world; but he was determined to become a disciple of the Lord and he felt impressed to study. Etienne had learned of this college as there had already been eleven students from his area who had studied there. The first one was Pawentaore Ouedraogo in 1968.

One of his fellow students during his year of studies was Norman Neill, from County Antrim in Northern Ireland. The two men became friends and spent time studying together. When it came to their summer break, Norman made plans to go home but unfortunately Etienne was unable to return to his homeland. Not wanting to leave him on his own, Etienne was invited to spend the summer with Norman's family and friends in Northern Ireland.

Etienne stayed in the home of Norman and Maureen Robinson, and he visited Antrim Elim Church where at that time Roy Kerr was the pastor. They really connected, and the couple formed such a connection with Etienne that they attended his graduation from the Institute at the end of his term.

Etienne's passion for his home country and people were evident. He really wanted to see his community transformed in the midst of desperate poverty. He returned home and continued to pour out his life, longing to see God's Kingdom come. He began to pastor in his local church. He trained up young leaders, and even established missionary work in neighbouring countries, particularly Benin.

Twenty-three years later, in 2001, Etienne received an invitation to attend a conference organised by Tearfund, to be held at Oxford University in England. The theme of the gathering was the development of Third World nations. He didn't know who had sent the invitation, but in order to accept it, he had to be able to pay his own way which he knew he was unable to do. Etienne was only earning $20 per month so there was no way he could afford the journey. However, a few weeks later, a pastor friend from Korea was visiting Burkina Faso and when he heard about the conference, he was that keen for Etienne to be there, he paid for his flights!

Etienne boarded the plane to the United Kingdom once more with great anticipation. When he arrived at the conference, his first question to the chairman present was: Who was responsible for sending out his invitation? They searched but they had no record of it; and, to this day, Etienne still does not know who or where it came from! When Maureen Robinson found out that Etienne was going to be back in England, not only did she cover the costs for his stay, but she also got him a plane ticket to come and visit his old friends in Northern Ireland.

During those 23 years, Roy Kerr had come down to help my granddad, in Richhill Elim, with some mission work in the village, and then he became a good friend of Drop Inn. Roy was delighted to hear that Etienne was coming back to Antrim: he called my Dad to see if he would come and meet his friend from Burkina Faso. When they met, Etienne shared about his city, how 3,000 kids had been orphaned as a result of AIDS and how his church wanted to help, but had no resources available.

Dad was deeply touched by his story, yet wondered what a small charity in Northern Ireland could do to minister to such a massive need in West Africa. However, early in 2003, Les accompanied Roy and a few others on a trip to Burkina Faso, to visit Etienne's city, Koudougou, and assess how we might offer some practical support. At this stage, Drop Inn were not in a financial position to take on any new projects. Our five shops were just covering the costs of our ongoing and most recent projects in Belarus, Ukraine and Albania, but the need was overwhelming and we had to do something. We were fully persuaded that James got it right when he said; *"Pure religion is to look after orphans and widows in their distress."* James 1:27 *NIV*

They were standing face-to-face with a huge need that required urgent attention; and also standing side by side with a man whose compassion and vision was contagious. Again, Drop Inn said 'Yes.' believing the step of faith into Burkina Faso would continue the momentum in Northern Ireland. On that trip, we committed to building a school to offer an education and feeding programme to 150 of the neediest in the city. In May of that same year, Dad travelled to Koudougou for his first visit. It was an exciting trip especially the day when many local dignitaries and media arrived at the site to witness the foundation stone being laid. The atmosphere was filled with hope and expectation as local builders began the work.

Before I continue to share how this work has grown, I want to introduce you to a special boy that caught Dad's attention in the middle of all the excitement. While Dad was 'turning the sod,' (breaking the ground for the new building) out of the corner of his eye he saw what he thought was an animal disappear around the side of a car. What eventually appeared in view was a young boy who had been born with two deformed legs and he spent his day trailing his little body round the dust and dirt of the town.

In the middle of everything else that was going on, it was a hopeless sight to witness. Dad left what he was doing and went to the boy. They couldn't communicate with each other, but he found out his name was Noufou: and in that moment Noufou was "seen." I'm convinced that, from the beginning, Father God has wanted to communicate to all of us that "I see you." In Exodus 3:7, we get an insight into the nature of God, when He communicates to Moses. Even when things are at their most hopeless and times are hard, I have seen and I have heard. As his ambassadors on earth, we want to be able to come alongside people in a way that says; "You are seen, you are heard."

The first thought that crossed Dad's mind was could we bring this boy to Northern Ireland to receive medical attention, as we had for kids in Eastern Europe. After sharing his heart with Etienne to see what could be done, Etienne was put in touch with a clinic in the capital city, Ouagadougou, that specialised in artificial limbs for kids. An appointment was made, and money was left with Etienne so Noufou could be brought to this clinic. It was wonderful to find out that this clinic were able to make artificial legs for him.

A few weeks later, this little six-year-old boy from a Muslim family, ignored and rejected by many after crawling on the ground for years, was standing in their mud hut on his new legs as a testimony to the kindness of God. The total cost was only £200. It is such a small price to offer dignity to this young boy and to give him a chance of a brighter future.

"I am sincerely grateful to Ronnie who has helped me since 2003. I was born without my complete legs. I could not walk, I was just crawling like an animal. But when this white man, Ronnie saw me in 2003 he had mercy on me even though he didn't know me. He passed support through Pastor Etienne and helped me to have artificial legs and I could now walk with my friends. With these artificial legs I have been able to go to school and I am heading to High School now. I can say that without Ronnie my life would have been a waste.

I was like an animal in 2003 but today I am walking like all men. God bless Mr Ronnie and his good friends!"

Noufou

It really is an honour to be involved in so many different nations and projects, being responsible for so many kids; but it's stories like Noufou's, that bring life to the words of Jesus in Matthew

25:40; *'Whatever you did for one of the least of these you did it to me.' NIV*

We have continually seen growth in our ministry, but never at the expense of missing the individuals on the edges of society. We don't want to ignore Jesus in the lives of the most needy and vulnerable.

Life, hope, purpose and potential...

After laying the foundation stone in May, the school building was completed in September 2003 and our first school was opened in Koudougou. After working out the ongoing costs of employing teachers and cooks, and purchasing supplies to run the school, we found that each child can be put through our school programme for £10 per month. This is a relatively small amount for most of us; but the impact it has on the future and destiny of these children is massive.

At our European conference in 2005, Etienne spoke of how the programme was running and then shared how widows in their community had been bringing their kids to see if they could get a place in the school. They were desperate to be able to get an education for them, but unfortunately Etienne had to tell them one by one that the rooms were at full capacity. He then had to watch as one by one they would walk away in tears. We could feel his anguish so it wasn't long until we built three extra classrooms for another 150 children. We are so thankful to the churches and individuals who have committed to sponsoring these children. Through this support we have been able to extend the programme to various locations and currently have over 600 children going through primary school education.

As the years went by, we sent teams to visit the schools and helped run summer kids' camps. Etienne was the type of man who had never asked for anything but would quietly pray and trust God to provide what they needed. In 2010, on the same site as the primary school and the church, we were able to build and open a secondary school. What was once dry, barren ground is now filled with life and hope, with purpose and potential.

It is a testimony to our teachers that the results in our schools are among the highest in the country. Parents who are in a position to afford education wanted to pay to have their kids educated in our schools but the commitment we made at the beginning remains the same. We serve a place for kids who have lost parents and the families of those who can't afford government education.

In 2014, one of the children who was part of Etienne's church family was admitted to hospital. During his stay Etienne visited and was shocked by what he saw. The boy was sharing a hospital bed with three other children. Yes: you read that correctly; a bed, not a ward! In a hospital room of four beds, Etienne counted 16 children, and they were being treated with different illnesses. Etienne stood alongside the family doing his best to offer words of comfort and encouragement but as he left the hospital grounds he began to weep and pray. As tears and words flowed together, a deep desire grew in Etienne's heart to be able to do something more to help people in their community.

The idea of a medical centre was birthed in the months of prayer that followed. The dream was to provide a facility for families where they could access local health care and would have space to care for the sick and their families in their most vulnerable moments.

After he had spent months praying, the question was asked; *'What is God saying now?'* Etienne shared what God had placed in his heart, and he didn't have to wait too long before an ideal piece of land was purchased. Once again, local builders got to work on creating a facility for people that would mean they would no longer have to choose whether to travel for medical help or feed their family.

I've already mentioned Alex from Ukraine. After hearing the reports from Burkina Faso, Alex wanted to be involved in helping the work that had started; so he brought a team from Ukraine to be a blessing to the wider family in Burkina Faso. They worked hard building the wall around the property.

It is a privilege to partner with people like Etienne. His enthusiasm and affection was so tangible as he shared his story with me. Every time he reflects on all God has done, he is *still* amazed. He is so grateful for the doors that have opened to bring the hope of Jesus into his community. He still considers the consequences of receiving an invitation from an unknown person to come to England in 2001, and what he could have missed out on if he had stayed at home.

For as I long as I can remember, my dad and Etienne have affectionately referred to each other as 'twin brothers.' He will regularly call me and my sister to ask how his *'white grandchildren'* are doing. The relationship with Etienne and his family and all our children in Burkina Faso is a constant reminder to me of how Jesus redefined family. In the gospels, Matthew 12:48 records Him asking the question: *'Who is my mother, and who are my brothers?'* and He answers his question when looking around the crowd; *'Here are my mother and my brothers! Whoever does God's will is my brother and sister and mother.'* Mark 3:32-35 *NIV*

I love the words of Bruxy Cavey used in his book, *'**The End of Religion**;'* *"Jesus opposes the idea that birth, blood and biology define true family. Instead He stresses that our unity with God and one another comes through shared faith and common purpose. In this way Jesus invites us to become part of a worldwide, transnational, multi-ethnic family of faith."*

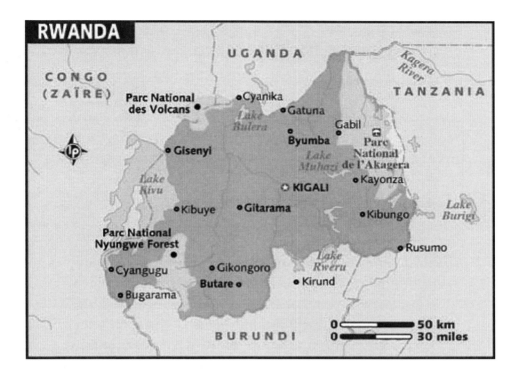

Capital - Kigali
Major religion - Christianity
Official Language - Rwanda; French; English
Population - 11,262,564
Currency - Rwandan franc (RF)

Rwanda is a beautiful country: a landlocked republic lying south of the Equator in east-central Africa. Known for its breathtaking scenery, Rwanda is often referred to as *le pays des mille collines*. (French: "land of a thousand hills") The capital is Kigali, located in the centre of the country on the Ruganwa River.

As in Burundi, the major ethnic groups in Rwanda are Hutu and Tutsi, respectively accounting for more than four-fifths and about one-seventh of the total population. The Twa, a hunter-gatherer group, constitute less than one percent of the population. Other minorities include a small group of Europeans (mostly missionaries, employees of relief and development programmes, and entrepreneurs), a small number of Asian merchants, and Africans from Tanzania, Uganda, the Democratic Republic of the Congo, and elsewhere.

Social differences between the Hutu and Tutsi traditionally were profound, as shown by the system of patron-client ties (*buhake*, or "cattle contract") through which the Tutsi, with a strong pastoralist tradition, gained social, economic, and political ascendancy over the Hutu, who were primarily agriculturalists. The formerly more distinct pastoral and agricultural systems have become well integrated, and nearly all farm households now engage simultaneously in crop and livestock production. During the Hutu revolution that began in late 1959, some 150,000 to 300,000 Tutsi were forced out of the country, which thus reduced the former ruling aristocracy to an even smaller minority. Since the end of the 1994 genocide, many Tutsi have returned to Rwanda to reclaim their heritage.

CHAPTER NINE

An invitation to Rwanda...

The singing group from Belarus continued to provide a platform to share what God was doing across the world through the Drop Inn family. On a visit to Kilsyth, Scotland, after the group had finished singing, Dad spoke about the developing work in Burkina Faso. At the end of the meeting, a man called Callum Henderson shared with Dad about a similar work he was doing in Rwanda in partnership with an organisation called Solace Ministries, and invited Dad to come and visit.

Less than ten years had passed since the genocide in Rwanda which, horrifically, saw up to one million people killed over a period of 100 days. Jean Gakwandi is a man who has survived this tragic time in Rwanda's history.

Jean's story is remarkable. The Rwandan president's plane was shot down on 6th April 1994 and early the next morning Jean, his wife Viviane and four children were awoken early by the sound of screaming friends and neighbours who were being slaughtered to death! Jean took his family to hide in a small store room in their house, and prayed that God would confuse and blind their attackers. They shot open the locks and fired through every window in the house; and when they failed to see any sign of life, they left. For almost two full days, Jean and his family lay still, having nothing to eat or drink until they were picked up and rushed to the home of a couple who were willing to risk their lives to shelter them. The killing came closer to the place they were hiding. Over and over again they experienced miraculous provision. At one point, after four days without food, Jean and his four-year-old daughter Jessie were hiding in a tiny cupboard when they felt something drip on them from above. It was chocolate that had been left in the top shelf of the cupboard by the family who had previously lived there. On another occasion, after a huge explosion outside, they found avocados at their front door step that had blown off a nearby tree in the blast!

After three months of hiding, Jean and his family walked free. Only then did they realise the full horror of what had taken place around them. Jean's mother had been attacked with a machete and left bleeding for days before she died. His 98-year-old grandmother was burned to death, his father killed with a sword, and 99 relatives on his father's side murdered. They were left feeling numb. In the months that followed, God began to do an incredible work of healing in Jean's heart, as he opened his heart for God to heal; and with healing came forgiveness.

As a result, Solace Ministries was established in 1995, dedicated to meeting the needs of widows and orphans. They were committed to a holistic process involving community development, medical care education and employment for those who are able. Their goal is to become an alternative family of survivors, restoring their dignity and creating networks of support for individuals who are traumatised, lonely, poor, and desiring hope as they face an uncertain future. The call they received from God was from Isaiah 40:1; *"Comfort, Comfort my people, says your God." NIV*

In 2004, Dad and Les made their first visit to Rwanda. They met Jean and Vivian and the Solace team and were inspired to partner with this ministry to bring comfort to the hurting. They visited different regions throughout the country. Every place they went, they met widows who had survived but had been left with physical and emotional scars. They had seen things that no mother or wife should ever have to see. Many were now raising children but had no regular source of income.

During the week, as Jean continued to share his vision, Dad saw the potential of regional centres that would serve as a family home for many, giving them a place where the women could meet and get trained in various activities and learn new skills. We wanted to empower the vision of Solace by creating facilities that would help women use their newly-acquired skills to generate income for their families.

Plans were soon put into place to build three regional centres, one in Nyanza in the southern province, one in Nyamata in the eastern province and the third in Kabuga, in rural Kigali. These centres have become a place of refuge in each of the communities. The buildings were built to a high standard so that they could be rented out for weddings, conferences and other activities. This allows the projects to become self-sustaining and increases potential income for the growing work of Solace.

As we have partnered with people in different places around the world in concrete, practical ways, it truly does allow them to dream

71

bigger dreams and pray bigger prayers. By 2007, they began to dream of a HIV/aids clinic in Kabuga.

This is how Jean summarises our partnership; *"To work together with Drop Inn has impacted and shaped Solace Ministries in a special way. The approach of partnership based on mutual trust is so inspiring. Through Drop Inn, we are ourselves comforted in order to be enabled to continue with the mission the Lord has entrusted to us to comfort others. The ministry can survive now with the assets provided by Drop Inn. Living a practical Christianity, the policy of Drop Inn, has helped Solace ministries to adopt the same ethos to implement the vision to 'Comfort His people' in a more comprehensive way for the glory of our God alone."*

Relentless for the sake of others...

Since 2001, the people of Ballymoney, Northern Ireland have raised a remarkable amount of money for our projects around the world. Their generosity has been instigated by the hard work and dedication of Edwina Chambers and her team, who are wonderful ambassadors of Drop Inn in their community.

Edwina's husband Bertie had died in July 2000. It was in the early part of 2001 that we were in the process of opening a shop in Ballymoney and Les asked Edwina, who was local to the area, if she would help us out by running the shop until we found someone else. Actually, we are really glad we never found anyone, as Edwina continues to run the shop to this day!

It was a Drop Inn team visit to Rwanda that inspired Edwina's commitment to raising as much money as she could. The widows she met in Rwanda had gripped her heart as they shared their stories of what they experienced in the genocide, and the life of poverty they now faced. Edwina has a way of noticing individuals on the edges, sitting with those on their own, offering them a hug to remind them that they are seen, even, on one occasion, going so far as giving the shoes on her feet when she found out they were a luxury one lady couldn't afford!

She came home from that first trip determined to do what she could to make a difference. Gathering volunteers, she simply began street collections, sponsored walks, quiz sheets and many more things. She engaged the community with fashion shows, auctions and various events. It wasn't long before she was able to send £100,000 for the vital building of Solace centres in different parts of Rwanda that we had committed to building as a community hub of activity and learning for widows. Her unashamed relentlessness for the sake of other people has been an inspiration to many.

When Edwina discovered the difficulties people who lived in outlying areas faced in getting medical care, she applied to the Police Federation of Northern Ireland for funds to purchase a jeep that could be used as an ambulance for the patients who lived in hard-to-reach places. They got in touch with Toyota: a new jeep was bought and delivered to our partners in Rwanda. Edwina then visited Burkina Faso, and her big heart still had the capacity to be touched by the needs she encountered there. Once again she rallied the people of Ballymoney to raise money for church buildings and to provide much-needed wells for different communities where access to clean water was very limited.

73

In 2017, Sandra, who was one of the shop volunteers, passed away. She wanted the money in lieu of flowers to be given towards a well in Burkina Faso. Sandra's Well was dedicated in 2018 on the site of our clinic. This well is different from the many others we have dedicated, because this depth of water at the site is not found very often. They have access to more than double the amount of water usually sourced. Pastor Etienne told us they could even begin to sell the water and still never be able to finish it. He says it is only by the grace of God. Sandra's favourite Bible story was the woman at the well; and the words Jesus speaks to the woman seem prophetic for this site; *"The water I give will be an artesian spring within gushing fountains of endless life."* John 4:14 *MSG*

Edwina's fundraising efforts show no sign of slowing down. At the time of writing she is gathering money for another well in Burkina Faso, this time in honour of my granny, who she acknowledges was an inspiration to her, as the person who opened our first charity shop 25 years ago. Edwina says working in the shop and visiting the nations has been a lifesaver to her; but I would say her work in the shop and visiting the nations has been a lifesaver to thousands!

CHAPTER TEN

Another significant connection...

Due to the increasing popularity of our summer mission adventures, Dad decided he would try and get his bus licence, which would allow us to bring more than 40 young people at a time across Europe. He was advised to go and train with a man called Robert Ferry who had a driving school just outside Dungannon. Robert and Dad spent a week to prepare Dad to take his tests. To relieve the tension in the long days, Dad would share his motivation for getting his licence and about the humanitarian aid work across Eastern Europe.

Years previously, Robert had spent time driving in and around Germany. At the end of their week together, he offered his services if Drop Inn ever needed a driver. Inevitably, it wasn't long before Robert was behind the steering wheel, ready to take a bus of volunteers to visit our projects in Belarus. Dad was happy that Robert was in the driving seat on that occasion. While they were driving through a snowstorm in Germany, they were involved in a bad accident when an overtaking car slid into the side of the bus. Robert had the experience to bring the bus to a safe stop. The bus was damaged and a rear tyre burst; but again with Robert's experience he was able to change the wheel in a nearby McDonald's car park while the rest of the group had their lunch!

We would have been wrong to assume this experience would have put Robert off. On his return home he said; *"Even though it wasn't the best journey, I was bitten anyway!'* Something had taken hold of him on this trip that left its mark! Our bus ended up being written off. Robert offered to supply the vehicles and help with the driving anytime, which was a huge blessing to Drop Inn.

That is only the beginning of his story. On one of the trips in 2005, Robert was once again driving. He had arranged to stop at a service station in England to pick up a lady he had recently met. This was the first time we met Lois, originally from Zambia but working as a midwife in Wigan. This was another one of those times: we never thought, after meeting this shy, quietly spoken lady, how she would become such an integral part of our lives.

Robert and Lois got married and lived in Northern Ireland. Lois learned more about the work of Drop Inn in Eastern Europe but was increasingly interested in the school project in Burkina Faso. Robert had been on many visits with us to Europe but they both came to Burkina Faso which proved to be another significant trip. It was here that the faith Lois had as a young girl growing up in Zambia was reignited, and where a passion was stirred in her to do something for vulnerable kids in her home nation.

In 2010, they went back to Zambia with the intention of seeing where they could bring *hope, help and healing*. They visited Kasama, in the north of the country. This is where Lois had been raised and educated. On this visit, one of Lois' nieces introduced her to a lady called Catherine, who was running a school out of a small hut. Catherine, a young disabled lady, was on her own, serving 129 vulnerable kids in the heart of her community. Robert and Lois initially proposed building a two-classroom school for her, and Drop Inn immediately got behind their vision to build a permanent school in one of the most deprived areas of the city.

Mum and Dad made their first visit to Zambia in May 2011 and set up support for teachers. They purchased much-needed reading and writing material alongside a feeding programme for the kids. Dad and Les visited again the following year as more doors were opening, because of the heart Robert and Lois had to see where help was most needed. The vision for what was possible in Zambia was widening. They made plans to build a school with three classrooms in a place called Kalikeka, which is 80km from Kasama. As relationships developed within this community, the responsibility of the school was handed over to the local people.

In 2014, a site was purchased to build a house on what would become a base for all the developing projects in Zambia. This would be home for Robert and Lois during the nine months of the year they would be there overseeing the building of the new school and involving themselves in other income-generating projects, mostly focused around farming. It was in February 2015 that work on a bigger school than initially planned in Kasama started: it was ready for the kids to move into the following February.

Dad had the absolute honour of officially opening the school in June 2016. To date, there are 800 of the most vulnerable kids in Kasama who are getting clothed, fed and educated, mostly because of the sacrifice of this incredible couple; but also because of people across the world who have sponsored these beautiful children. What we are able to do is because of their generosity. In order to be able to do the same for more kids, it simply needs more people to commit to the £10 a month: this allows kids in difficult parts of the world the chance to learn, the opportunity to thrive and the permission to dream.

In the Drop Inn family, Robert and Lois continue to inspire us. They are now in their 70's and have yet to show any signs of slowing down. In fact all we see is an increased determination and the grace to work even harder. We have had front row seats to watch a dream being birthed and come to life while also witnessing a couple come alive in the plans and purposes of God.

'For we are God's masterpiece. He has created us anew in Christ Jesus, so we can do the good things he planned for us long ago.'
Ephesians 2:10 NLT

Stepping forward in the plans and purposes of God...

CHAPTER ELEVEN

Partnering across the islands...

As I have already mentioned, one of the ways we shared the story of what we were doing in Belarus was to tour many parts of the UK with the singing group from the Chernobyl region. During the tour of Northern Ireland and the mainland, we ventured across the water. In January 1998, the group included a visit to Ramsey on the Isle of Man. The concert took place in the local grammar school. In the audience that night were Steve and Alison Taylor who were there after their daughter had persuaded them to come and hear the songs and stories from Belarus.

Alison was a nurse with Hospice and Steve worked for the Steam Packet Company on the island. That night as they listened to Dad sharing the stories from the hospitals and orphanages that we were working into, Steve's heart was touched. In response to the invitation to anyone who wanted to visit, Steve made himself available; though he didn't even have a passport! A few months later, Steve was in Minsk, capital city of Belarus. It was a visit to the cerebral palsy hospital in particular that broke his heart. The staff did not even have the most basic equipment to meet the needs of the young boys and girls that were being cared for. He was also aware there were no colourful pictures hanging on the walls, there were no teddies in the children's beds. It was here that Steve realised the importance of bringing teams to visit real life people and real-life projects.

It's one thing to tell a story or show a photograph, but it's something else to sit alongside the poor and the sick, look them in the eye and be moved with compassion.

Steve returned to the Isle of Man, determined to do what he could to make a difference. He shared his experience with Alison. The following year she travelled with him and, owing to her passion and experience in healthcare, they spent a week in the hospital for children with cerebral palsy. On her first visit to the surgical ward, she sat with a five-year-old girl who was dying; and there was no antibiotic to help her. Alison spent much of her week simply loving and caring for this little girl and many others. In response to her time with these incredible children, she came home with the same resolve as Steve to do whatever she could to make a difference. She knew that she couldn't see the need and do nothing about it.

One of the biggest events that takes place in the Isle of Man every year is the TT motorcycling races. To make a start on raising money, they set up a stall to sell soup with a roll to people passing by during the TT week. On the first occasion they raised £38: and so began their Belarus Fund.

In much the same way as momentum had gathered in Northern Ireland a few years earlier, it was now happening on the Isle of Man too. Steve and Alison began to bring people from other churches on the island to be a part of the group visits. They continued with fundraising events and shared the story with many others. By

2002, they had raised £10,000 for a badly-needed kitchen in an orphanage in Izarichi, Belarus.

Steve was making good use of his newly-published passport. On one of his earliest visits, he met Les. As the projects increased across Eastern Europe, it meant there were more lorry loads of humanitarian aid being sent out each year. There was a need for more drivers and, once again, Steve made himself available. Because of his continued availability, he has taken over 25 loads of *hope, help and healing to a hurting world.*

Steve and Alison were still working their full-time jobs, yet continued to gather support for projects beyond Europe. They bought a dairy cow for Etienne and the kids in Burkina Faso; they blessed what Nigel was doing in Venezuela; and sent hundreds and hundreds of shoeboxes for us to distribute in Belarus and Ukraine every year.

Things were developing quickly in Rwanda. Les and Carol Ann had taken responsibility for group visits and communication about the projects and finances. In 2007, Les needed someone to go to Rwanda and had asked Alison to consider going. Her initial response was one of fear. She was happy to raise money but didn't want to be sent to Africa! In spite of her fears, when she heard that Solace wanted to build a clinic, it helped convince her that she was the ideal person to go.

Solace had been involved in medical work since 2004, mainly addressing the needs of women and young girls affected by HIV/ AIDS, because of the sexual violence during the genocide. They had set up a care and treatment scheme for 800 women who suffered from the disease. In Rwanda the Department for International Development financed a five-year care and treatment project that was helping 2800 people affected by HIV/AIDS. As the project was being phased out in 2010, there were almost 350 still on the treatment. Solace knew it was necessary to continue to encourage enrolment into their HIV treatment programme, through testing, confidentiality, education, pre and post-test counselling and trauma counselling.

The support given to these patients highlighted other unmet needs, which are barely accessible to poor people in general and in particular to widows and orphans. It became a pressing need to create somewhere that would enable Solace Ministries to carry on these activities as well as responding to the needs of the people who were unable to receive the treatment in the five-year project. After hearing the vision and meeting the people who were in most need of medical care, Alison pledged £25,000 to the building of medical clinic in Kabuga. Back in the Isle of Man, they had £10,000 in the bank, where would the remaining money come from that she had pledged?

It wasn't long after returning home from her visit to Rwanda that Steve and Alison made the decision to open their first Drop Inn shop. The building work of the clinic began in 2008, and with the income from the shop and various sponsors, it was completed in 2010. It was then officially opened in March 2011 by Rwanda's Minister of Health, alongside a team from Drop Inn.

The clinic had been assigned to care for a population of more than 45,000 people; and many more from further away were requesting the services that were being provided.

In the words of the Solace team; *"The Solace Medical Clinic was built in Kabuga by Drop Inn, Isle of Man. They have deeply impacted the vision of Solace Ministries to serve and comfort the suffering. We humbly recognise the hard work of Steve and Alison Taylor and their team in the Isle of Man which is bearing much fruit for the glory of God. Thousands of children, women and men have had their health saved in this clinic."*

When Alison went back to visit the clinic the following year, they had already outgrown the facility. It was clear they needed a bigger place. There was a need to increase care for children, a need for a maternity unit and space for a family planning clinic. When a twenty-bed hospital was suggested, Alison thought there was no way they were taking that on. But at the time of writing, the hospital is almost ready to open, thanks to the compassion and dedication of Steve and Alison, who, along with the people of the Isle of Man, (including the Isle of Man government) have sent over £250,000 to *bring hope, help and healing to a hurting nation.*

Coming together as one…

'*For just as each of us has one body with many members, and these members do not all have the same function, so in Christ we, though many, form one body, and each member belongs to all the others.'* Romans 12:4-5 *NIV*

The number of projects grew and the friendship circles in each nation widened as more pastors were being supported. It became increasingly difficult to maintain communication and even more difficult to visit everyone. One of the highlights of the year is when we get as much of the Drop Inn family together as possible. We have gatherings each October in Europe and meet in India during November. Our annual conference in Europe and Asia gave us the opportunity to get everybody in one place for one week. These times have been important for Mum and Dad, but we now also have the joy of seeing the family of God connecting with one another, worshipping together and learning together. It is a time to *'encourage one another and build each other up.'* 1 Thessalonians 5:11 NIV

We have great times of worship, and the finest Bible teaching, with our long-time friends Eugene and Darla Smith. But the most exciting thing to come from these times is the strong reminder that as part of the family of God, *'we belong to one another'* and hearing how it is being lived out in a practical way.

I have heard it being said; *'The Kingdom moves at the speed of relationships.'* Well, I can definitely testify to that! As relationships have deepened over the years around the world we have truly seen the Kingdom advance. One of those relationships has been with Eugene and Darla Smith. Dad first heard Eugene preach in 1997. Eugene and his wife Darla were leading an International worship and teaching ministry from their home in Canada. A friendship was formed shortly afterwards; then Eugene became involved with the work and travelled with Dad on parts of the Belarus singing group tour in Northern Ireland. Following that, Eugene began to travel with Dad and the teams to all the places we had projects: initially in Belarus, Albania and Burkina Faso; but almost everywhere else since. This was a chance for us to not only support local churches and their communities in a practical way but to better equip them with life-giving Bible teaching.

As Eugene had travelled extensively, he became our point of connection with future partnerships in Ukraine and Haiti. He shared this quotation with me; *'Anyone can count the seeds in an apple but only God can count the number of apples in a seed.''* Essentially, small beginnings can bring huge results. It's hard to measure what can come from small seeds; the seed of one friendship made, or the seed of one connection made. Where Eugene had brought his teaching ministry, we were able to complement that with practical ministry.

In 2005, Dad and Les, alongside Drop Inn board member Neville Garland, made their first visit to Haiti with Eugene, who had been travelling into Haiti since 1997. He introduced us to Pastor Lesley Bertrand, with whom we have partnered from that trip. Eugene had been exposed to the huge need in this country and instinctively wanted to help. He established a kids' sponsorship programme which he found difficult to sustain. I appreciate Eugene's humility as he recognises that there is a skill-set that we had, but he didn't. Equally, we have been incredibly blessed as we have brought Eugene to operate in the skill-set he has that we don't.

Eugene said; *"I looked for others to take over various aspects of our work in Haiti that freed me up to focus my attention on teaching. Drop Inn Ministries immediately came to assist.*

"It was my privilege to lead a team from Drop Inn to Haiti with me one year, a new place where Ronnie could exercise his management skills in a much-needed area of the world. Drop Inn had the gifting and resources to do far beyond what I could do."

It's in 1 Corinthians 12 where Paul talks about this; *'There are different kinds of gifts but the same spirit distributes them, there are different kinds of service but the same Lord, there are different kinds of working but in all of them and in everyone it is the same God at work.' (v4-6) NIV*

It's another beautiful sign of partnership when we all use what's been given for the *common good*, *'a spiritual gift is given to each of us so we can help each other.' (v7) NLT*

As God opened doors for us in other parts of the world, Eugene would come and teach the Word of God to leaders and their churches. He has been our conference speaker at every European conference, except one since 2002, and every Asian conference since the first one in 2014. As we partner together, the Word is preached, then lived out; and when the Word is taught, then it becomes flesh.

Eugene says; *"By God's grace, doors to more and more countries opened to Drop Inn. As those doors opened, Ronnie and Carolyn graciously kept inviting me along to teach the Word of God to the churches and to the leaders. Drop Inn experienced steady, and at times, phenomenal growth as they learned through challenges and passed many tests of faith, where experience and hard-earned wisdom were gained.*

"In many ways, they have become an example of what can happen if we follow the God-given burdens of our hearts and yield ourselves to Him. A major part of that growth was the annual Drop Inn conference in Eastern Europe. Pastors and leaders that were supported by Drop Inn were brought together to a location in Europe for a week of refreshment, worship, teaching, sharing with one another and encouragement. Every year, except one, I have been asked to be the

main speaker. On several occasions, Darla has been able to accompany me as she led worship, with the help of the Belarussian choir.

"Some years later, as Drop Inn's boundaries grew ever larger, an annual Asian conference was added to the schedule. Once again, I am grateful to have been asked to serve there as well.

"From my personal perspective, my wife and I are deeply grateful for the open doors and opportunities Drop Inn have extended to us. These opportunities have helped to shape our own lives, outlook and world perspectives, challenged our faith, given us an example to emulate, and facilitated to sharpen whatever gifts God has chosen to endow us with."

It has been helpful for me to watch this mutual honouring of one another's personalities and gifting, to witness a genuine desire to build the Kingdom above their own brands or egos; and to recognise that we build better together.

Eugene comments; *"The investment Drop Inn has put into me is being expressed to others, many of whom Drop Inn has never personally met. Drop Inn's influence goes far beyond what their eyes can see. Along our pilgrimage through this world, God arranges a few key people to come into our lives. For us, among those few key people, Ronnie and Carolyn were and still are significant."*

As with Dad, Eugene's increasing burden is to be a mentor to the next generation. He is asking the same questions we are asking: *"How do we prepare for the future? Surely a ministry does not need to die with us? Surely a ministry ought to leave a legacy!"*

Eugene's thinking... *"There needs to be a conscious effort to raise sons and daughters to carry the work forward. Even from its early days, Drop Inn opened up its international outreaches to many people. People from all walks of life joined a Drop Inn team for a short-term outreach somewhere in the world. This had a two-fold effect. It was a help to the country that was visited, and those who made the trips had their own lives impacted in ways they couldn't have dreamed. But mentoring needs to be specific as well as general.*

"The young men who once pioneered develop into fathers. There are those that follow behind who carry a similar calling that need the voice of experience, that can witness the steadfastness of faith and determination, that observe both the challenges and joys involved in doing God's work. Moses had a Joshua. Elijah had an Elisha. Paul had Timothy and Titus."

CHAPTER TWELVE

Great gatherings...

Valentine, who is a pastor of a church in Miyouri, a small village in Belarus, met Dad in 2003 and was then invited to our European conference. At that time it was held in the Austrian Alps. The relationship with Valentine and his family continued to grow and he took on the role of pastor in his church in 2015.

He was from a small community and their church congregation was small. He admits they had developed a small mindset, believing they couldn't influence anything, anywhere. However, it was during the conference in 2015, when an invitation was made to support the work of those that were part of the worldwide Drop Inn family, that something happened in Valentine's heart. He realised they came every year to consume with no thought of giving back. In that moment, regardless of the amount of people that were in his church or amount of money they had in the bank, he knew they could give something. From that day Valentine and his church committed to supporting one of our school projects in India.

I love hearing Valentine tell the story of how their church has embraced this little school in India, and how it's caused them to see differently; looking outwards rather than inwards, rather than focusing on what they *don't* have and *can't* do. His testimony is that the church has been more inspired than what a year's worth of sermons could have done! Now there is a group of people who, despite never travelling beyond the limits of their home city, are known 3500 miles away in India!

Alex is another pastor in Belarus who has got caught up in the bigger picture of God's Kingdom advancing across the world. Dad met Alex in 2001 on one of Drop Inn's regular shoebox visits to the rehab centre in Rudnya. After years of addiction, he began his training to become a church pastor. He wanted people to experience the freedom that he now walked in. His desire was to come alongside people who had been in the same place he had been, caught in the same cycles that he knew all about.

In 2007, in the church where he was serving, he was meeting with so many people that they needed their own building to set up a rehab centre of their own. Seven years after meeting Alex for the first time as a participant in rehab, Drop Inn made up the amount of money that was needed to purchase the building for a rehab centre that Alex was now going to be responsible for leading.

Alex was invited to our European conferences. Each year he would hear mission reports of what God was doing through the Drop Inn family in many parts of the world. His heart was stirred with each story he would hear. It was exciting for us to watch as he built good relationships with friends in Pridnestrovia and Latvia, and began partnering with church leaders to see rehab centres opening in various locations. We are grateful that we could offer Alex the platform to develop this important ministry across Eastern Europe.

91

In 2013, Alex and his wife went to Turkey with Mum and Dad and a few other married couples. They went to seek direction from the Lord for their next step. Travelling to this part of the world was a challenge for Alex. Before coming to faith in Jesus, he was very negative towards Arabs and had treated them poorly. Even after coming to faith in Jesus he still admitted to feelings of indifference, with no interest in engaging with them.

A couple of years later, he went with Dad to Israel. As he met with Arab Christians in Palestine, something began to change in his heart. It was on this same trip that he met Homero, who we partner with in Jordan. As he listened to Homero tell his story of what God was doing in the Middle East, how people from Iraq, Syria, and Egypt had to run for refuge because of the danger they were facing in their own communities, Alex repented of what he felt had been a hypocritical attitude and his heart was absolutely transformed.

He was no longer indifferent. He wanted to meet these people, to serve them and to love them. He became so moved by what these people were going through that he made his first trip to Jordan to help the team bring hope to hopeless situations.

It is currently his dream to open a Drop Inn centre in the Middle East. Alex speaks of how God has used relationships with Drop Inn, particularly Mum and Dad, to influence his family. All their mission work through the church is on the platform that Drop Inn provides. In their church they have developed a prayer group of 52 faithful prayer warriors who pray for projects and nations Drop Inn represent. Even though many of them may never get the opportunity to travel, they realise their responsibility towards one another as part of the one body. It has been a remarkable journey from rehab to now. Alex and his wife remain open to what God wants for them and from them.

Ministering in the Middle East...

It was in June 2014 that Dad had a significant conversation on Skype. A young man called Homero, his wife Deborah and two children, were preparing to leave their homeland of Brazil to serve God in Jordan. Homero spoke of the persecution in Iraq at that time, how ISIS were taking over all the Christian villages in Northern Iraq, and he spoke of his passion and vision to serve the suffering church in the Middle East. A few weeks after Homero and his family had settled in Jordan. Dad was their first visitor and joined them as they blessed Christian Iraqi refugees with welcoming kits which we were able to help finance. These kits contained mattresses, blankets, pillows and food parcels.

Over the years the work has continued to increase, and we have been able to partner with this beautiful family in a challenging part of the world. We continue to support their many and varied projects, and have brought Homero to share his story at our European conference. Pastors and leaders were moved with the reality of what was happening, so they invited Homero to speak in their churches. He was able to visit Belarus, Ukraine and Latvia, where he challenged the churches and Believers with the plight of the suffering church in the Middle East.

It is our joy to watch these churches that have received from Drop Inn for so long begin to give to those in need in Jordan; not only giving, but some even going to encourage, serve and love those who have had to flee with their families for their own safety. As Homero's dream has grown, so has the team around him. He has been able to send workers to spend three months with our team in Northern Ireland, where they serve alongside us while trying to improve their English.

We love investing in these young people who have given up their lives to be the hands and feet of Jesus in Jordan. The investment is worth even more when Homero reports that his team come back to Jordan transformed and better equipped to fulfil their calling.

Into the unknown...

In the spring of 2005, Dad visited Sergey Botez, who is the pastor of a church in a town called Pervomaisk. Prior to this visit, Dad had been in Ukraine. The man who was interpreting for him on this occasion asked if he had ever been to Pridnestrovia. I'm sure that, like many of you reading this, your response would have been the same as Dad's: that he'd never heard of it! It is also known as Transnistria. It is mostly an unrecognised state, a narrow strip of land between Ukraine and Moldova. Never had it been more true that Drop Inn was moving into unknown territory!

After being introduced to Sergey, Dad invited him to our annual European conference the following October. It was from this point that we began to serve together in order to see visible signs of Kingdom activity in a place that was invisible to many.

Relationships with our friends in Pridnestrovia have continued to develop over the years and the Drop Inn model has remained the same: to come alongside local churches with a heart for local community and resource them to be agents of transformation. Every Christmas the church is now able to give gifts to many children through our Christmas shoebox appeal. They are running camps for young people of all ages, which requires more pastoral care as the work continues in supporting them throughout the year. In response to what God has been doing, we have committed to sponsoring two more pastors. Every part of the world we have invested in has been with the intention of meeting the physical need as much as the spiritual need.

What that looks like presently is: every month, ten of the most needy families are receiving food packages. We are able to help boys and girls in an orphanage in a village called Chobruchi, and in the local schools. As with many of our projects in Eastern Europe, we are assisting in the work of the rehab centre. The signs of hope and life being restored in these centres across Eastern Europe are really encouraging.

In John's first letter, he gives us a beautiful definition of love from the example Jesus gave us to follow; *"This is how we know what love is - Jesus Christ laid down his life for us. And we ought to lay down our lives for our brothers and sisters. If anyone has material possessions and sees a brother or sister in need but has no pity on them, how can the love of God be in that person. Dear children, let us not love with words or speech, but with action and in truth."* 1 John 3:16-18 *NIV*

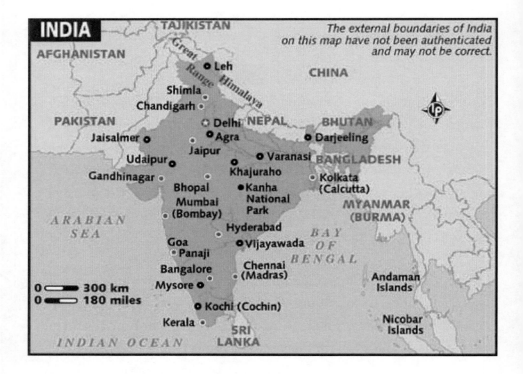

Capital - New Delhi
Major religion - Hindu
Official language - Hindi; English
Population - 1,293,057,000
Currency - Indian Rupee

India continues to develop at a rapid pace. It is a constitutional republic consisting of 29 states, each with a substantial degree of control over its own affairs; six less fully empowered union territories; and the Delhi national capital territory, which includes New Delhi, India's capital. With roughly one-sixth of the world's total population, India is the second most populous country, after China.

India remains one of the most ethnically diverse countries in the world. Apart from its many religions and sects, India is home to innumerable castes and tribes, as well as to more than a dozen major and hundreds of minor linguistic groups from several language families unrelated to one another. Religious minorities, including Muslims, Christians, Sikhs, Buddhists, and Jains, still account for a significant proportion of the population; collectively, their numbers exceed the populations of all countries except China. Earnest attempts have been made to instil a spirit of nationhood in so varied a population, but tensions between neighbouring groups have remained and at times have resulted in outbreaks of violence. Yet social legislation has done much to alleviate the disabilities previously suffered by formerly "untouchable" castes, tribal populations, women, and other traditionally disadvantaged segments of society.

CHAPTER THIRTEEN

Boldly sharing the love...

In 2006, Sunny, a young man from India, was visiting Armagh. Sunny had been told to get in touch with Dad to share about his ministry in Odisha, (formerly Orissa) an eastern Indian state on the Bay of Bengal. Sunny had been faithfully serving his community. He was feeding the hungry, providing shelter to the homeless and reaching out to unreached people in the northern part of India. After meeting Sunny and hearing his desire to see transformation in his city, we committed to supporting him and the work to which God had called him. Sunny says that, from this first conversation, he was welcomed into the Drop Inn family and has been nurtured and cared for ever since.

The work has grown over the years, as has Sunny's family. He married Kuni and they have two boys, Jack and Jimmy. The school they established for orphaned boys and girls had 20 children; but they had only two toilets and only two hours of running water a day. However, today they have 80 kids and 24-hour running water, and they now have teachers and staff to help take care of the children.

In parts of the world where it is difficult to be a Christian, we are blessed to partner with couples like Sunny and Kuni, who continue boldly to share the love of Jesus in such practical ways.

In Odisha's neighbouring state of West Bengal, we began a partnership with Anupam and his *Impact Asia* team in 2012. Anupam has a strong desire to serve the Lord in his Indian state, but also in the other Asian nations that surround him. He is perfectly placed to step into any of Bhutan, Bangladesh and Nepal, all bordering West Bengal.

Within their own community Anupam and his team opened *Papa's House*. This was to provide a home for orphaned kids and some of the most vulnerable kids in the region. There are currently 18 kids in Papa's House. We support this project financially, helping provide shelter, food, clothing, tuition and spiritual education. We are also able to send our interns each year to play with the kids, sing with them, and remind them how valued they truly are. In the southern part of India, in Hyderabad, we have been actively involved with a ministry called HOPE (Help for the Oppressed and Poor Empowerment) since 2014.

Let me introduce you to Pradeep. He was born with a hole in his heart and would often take seizures, when he would turn blue and his mother would carry him running to hospitals and churches. She prayed that if God healed her baby, she would commit him to God's ministry. During his childhood years Pradeep was miraculously healed. A few years later, he joined a Bible college and it was here that God gave him a burden to share the love of Jesus to Muslims. He did a three-year course on Islamic studies. When he left college, he learned basic Arabic and began a mercy ministry among Muslims in Hyderabad. As he was reaching out into the city, he was meeting children who were living on the streets alone.

I was personally really challenged by Pradeep's response to what he saw. He said; *"I had to rescue the street children; life should not be this way for these children."* He didn't hesitate to act: he couldn't ignore what was right in front of him. He opened a home for these children in 2003. His conviction was, they would not ask for or raise funds but would trust God for their daily personal and ministry needs. It wasn't long before they were taking care of 30 boys and girls.

Day after day, God provided amazingly for their needs. They had strangers bringing bags of rice right when they were at their last meal; and they had unknown people send donations for their needs right on time. At the time of writing, they are taking care of 35 orphaned kids. Many of these kids from the street are HIV affected, and have been abused and rejected. Pradeep testifies over and over again to the faithfulness of God in meeting their needs as they have cared for these children. Educational needs, rents, salaries, medical needs, groceries and protection have all been supplied in amazing ways.

Pradeep is married to Rebecca and they have two daughters, Shifa who is eight-years-old and Saachi, who is three. In 2018, God led them to move from Hyderabad to Maharashtra, a state in west-central India. They moved to work among the Korku people. These tribal people live in extreme poverty, with issues of hunger and malnutrition. Their homes are made of wood and grass. There is no hospital, no school, and no transportation for 30km. They have never heard the gospel.

There are many adults and children who die in this area from preventable diseases every year. Pradeep is teaching them health and hygiene skills. He is also bringing them medicines. He takes pictures of those who are sick and sends them to his friend, Dr Shankar in Hyderabad, along with details of their symptoms. Dr Shankar prescribes them medicines and Pradeep brings the medicines to them the next day. He has loved and served these people well and has gained their trust; and is now beginning to see God do amazing things among them.

At Christmas time, he invited all the villagers together, where they did a medical camp and then shared the gospel story with them. They are testifying that God is doing miracles among them, driving out demons; and these tribal people are increasingly opening their hearts to the Lord.

We love partnering with people in a way that releases them to further the call God has placed on their lives. We recognise there are things about certain cultures and traditions we will never fully understand, so to empower local people to minister to local people is really important to us. I love the way Pradeep acknowledges my mum and dad in our giving and our visiting, he said; *"They never acted as bosses, telling us to do ministry this way or that; but they would spend time with our children and pray with them. We praise God for Drop Inn and the sacrificial support they give regularly which helps us to serve God and show His love to the uncared and unwanted."*

It's always exciting for us when other Drop Inn staff take ownership of what we are all a part of. As the number of charity shops has increased over the years, we have needed vans and drivers to service these shops. Right across the country, our guys are collecting and delivering furniture every week. They play such an important role in how the ministry functions. One of our drivers is called Javier, or more commonly referred to as Puma. He is originally from Venezuela and was part of the team that worked alongside Nigel in Barquisimeto.

Puma visited our project in Burkina Faso in 2009, where he met Jenna. They fell in love, got married and are now living in Northern Ireland. Puma was on a Drop Inn visit to India in 2014 with my dad when we were first introduced to Pradeep. Pradeep has been so grateful for the ways Puma has encouraged them since then. Pradeep says; *"He laughed with us, cried with us and always asks for prayer requests and lifted us up, praise God for Puma and Jenna!"* This is friendship! We all need partners and supporters; but when it comes to living out the ways of Jesus, we want to do that with friends, mutually loving and serving one another, where no time, place or language is a barrier.

The untouchables…

Just 200km north of Hyderabad, there is a small village called Porandla. It is one of the oldest villages in India and has a population of just over 6,000 people. Like many Hindu villages across India, there is a caste system that divides people into different categories based on their social status. Those at the lowest end of this system are known as Dallits, or more commonly referred to as the *'untouchables.'*

In Porandla, these caste distinctions are very much evident, with the higher castes refusing to acknowledge those of a lower caste. It was into this place and this environment that God brought a man called Benjamin in the year 2000 to bring a message of hope to this previously unreached village.

No one had heard the story of Jesus, none of these 'untouchables' had heard of a God who would take on the nature of a servant who, with a touch of His hand, would open blind eyes, would heal the sick and set captives free. With one touch He would give dignity to those who were called unclean; would free those from the shame of being ignored and rejected. Benjamin moved in with his wife Ruth and began to share this gospel and as people responded, he planted a church which continues to meet every Sunday with currently over 70 people worshipping Jesus.

Not only had there been no Church or Kingdom witness in Porandla, there was none in the 700 villages that surrounded it. God gave Benjamin a burden to pray for these villages and that local missionaries would be raised up. I'm reminded of Matthew 9, where Jesus travelled through the villages announcing, 'the good news of the Kingdom.' We are told that 'when he saw the crowds, he had compassion on them because they were like sheep without a shepherd, so Jesus said to his disciples, "The harvest is great but the workers are few, so pray to the Lord who is in charge of the harvest, ask him to send more workers into his fields."' Matthew 9:36-38 NLT

We met Benjamin in 2015 and he has been part of the Drop Inn family ever since. As we have partnered together, there are now twelve missionaries who have been raised up and equipped to help Benjamin sow seeds of love into these villages that are beginning and will continue to reap a harvest. We truly count it a joy to be able to support these missionaries and their families as they lay down their lives so that others would find life in Jesus.

The Turning Point...

Reuben Pradhan was born in Shillong in the north-east of India. He was from a Hindu background but in 1989, alongside his parents, he gave his life to Jesus. It was in that same year that he graduated from college and joined a short-term mission work in a remote village for several months. When he returned home to his own community, he planted a church with his mum and dad, which he would pastor for the next 20 years. During this time he married Anu and they had five children.

Nepal was in fact Reuben's ancestral home and for years had felt God was preparing him and his family to establish a Kingdom work there. In 2010, he left India with his family and began to serve existing churches in the nation. He got involved in teaching in the Bible schools, reaching out to students and running the training for the Alpha Course. It was in his second year of their time in Nepal when Reuben was introduced to Drop Inn.

Dad and a close friend of the ministry, Davy Grey, came to visit just at the time Reuben and his family were struggling financially. In answer to their prayer, we were able to come alongside them and lovingly support them to further develop their ministry. In 2015, they made the strategic decision to move back to India but close to the border in a town called Siliguri in the state of West Bengal. This is the state that shares a border with Bhutan and

Bangladesh. This move allowed Reuben to not only reach people from different Indian communities but also nationals from these neighbouring countries.

After moving to Siliguri, the Lord opened the door for Reuben to bring the Good News of Jesus to addicts and alcoholics in a non-Christian rehab centre. He has seen many come to faith and continues to watch many of their lives being transformed. Reuben is a born evangelist. He is reaching out to people far from Jesus in his region by doing intentional weekly street evangelism. Reuben and his team have had people respond immediately to Jesus in the middle of the road; they have seen some beautiful healing take place. As a result, in May 2018 they started a bilingual church (English/Hindu) called *The Turning Point*.

Hyderabad, India...

In 2012, we began partnering with Stephen David and his ministry in Hyderabad, Southern India.

Several months before we met Stephen in person, Davy Grey connected with him online after commenting on a sermon on YouTube that they were both watching. Davy was on staff, supervising our intern programme. After a few conversations, Davy and I went to visit Stephen in his home. We heard about his heart for the church and for his country to walk in the ways of Jesus. After spending a day with Stephen, his family and his team, we felt a genuine heart-connection, believing the Lord was opening a door for deeper relationship. A few months later, Dad was in India and came to spend some time with Stephen. We have partnered with him to this day, helping orphans and supporting church planters among the numerous people receiving help.

I asked Stephen to introduce himself...

"I am Stephen David. I serve the Lord in South India. I am a pastor of a church which I started by God's grace. I write songs of praise and worship. I preach and teach God's word. I speak in conferences and seminars. I write tracts, articles, booklets, workbooks and books to encourage people. I love discipling and helping people. My life has been tremendously used by the Lord to be a great blessing to many people.

"What's the need for me to share the above description of myself? Am I trying to show off? No. The reason for my sharing is to let you know that none of the above works is possible if the Lord had not brought Drop Inn into my life.

"A few years ago, I was at a crossroad wondering how I go ahead in the ministry the Lord has given me. I was enormously helpless and confused. The Lord had blessed me with wonderful gifts but I needed God's help to use what God has given me to serve people. It was at this time that I happened to meet David Grey and Neil Dawson for the first time in Hyderabad."

He continues, *"One of the glorious events we look forward to every year is the Drop Inn Asia conference. How much encouragement and support Drop Inn pours into this conference to stir up Christian workers in Asia to continue to serve the Lord!*

"Ronnie is a man of simplicity and humility, his wife Carolyn is a woman who is always filled with the joy of the Lord. My team

and I have been amazingly blessed through their lives about whose investment the heaven would greatly testify on the Last Day."

Southeast Asia....

Unfortunately for security purposes we can't share the name of the country, so we will just refer to it as Southeast Asia. It was in March 2013 that Mum and Dad visited Erwin Balany and his wife Dawna in a part of Southeast Asia, and were amazed at the ministry they were leading. This was the beginning of a great partnership.

This is what Erwin had to say:

"Drop Inn Ministries has been a faithful ministry partner to us. Through its partnership, we are able to do what God has called us to do, which is to advance God's kingdom in a country in Southeast Asia through world missions, church planting, and campus ministries.

"As a cross-cultural missionary, we consider Drop Inn Ministries as a major sending-partner. It is through its partnership we are able to lead a church planting initiative in a country in Southeast Asia, which is a predominantly Buddhist and a creative-access nation, where preaching of the gospel is prohibited.

"Because of the faith-restrictions in the country, we put up a cafe, a church in disguise of a cafe. It is where the church meets for corporate worship every Sunday and where the church does discipleship activities during weekdays. By the grace of God, the Lord is continually using the cafe to advance His work and protect His people from persecution."

What an amazing couple! We love their bold faith in the middle of such challenges. They are actively reaching out to university students, understanding they are the future leaders of the country; and believing that when they change the campus, they change the world. It is encouraging for us to hear the church is continuously growing in number. It is now being led by locals and even becoming a blessing to the surrounding nations.

Erwin continues; *"Drop Inn not only partner with us financially but also in prayer. It is certainly making a great impact for Christ in the lives of many people, especially among students in a country in Southeast Asia."*

Pakistan....

On 1st November 2013, Mum and Dad went to Pakistan for the first time. This was a part of the world they had been praying about for a long time. Through a mutual friend, they were meeting Emmanuel Faraz in the city of Multan to spend four days on the ground with him and his ministry. It was an amazing experience, both culturally and spiritually. From that we have been able to bless the work there. Our support is helping to run a school, a church and a beauty parlour. The beauty parlour is a place they have opened for young girls in the most deprived parts of the community. The future for many of these girls is bleak; but through the training programme provided, it opens doors of opportunities for them that otherwise don't exist.

Emmanuel told me; *"Through this beauty parlour training programme, 53 girls have accepted Jesus as their saviour, and we are winning young souls for His Kingdom. It's a real honour and pleasure to be working with Ronnie, Carolyn and Drop Inn.*

"We do our best for the empowerment of women. For this we are running a beauty parlour, where we train young girls so that they can get some skills to earn money. There is one young widow from a poor family: she is 24-years-old and her name is Nabila. She has two daughters, aged three and four. She is working in our parlour from last year and we are paying her a good salary each month. When she first came into the parlour, she was just nominally Christian; but while working with the church she accepted Lord Jesus Christ as her personal Saviour. She always acknowledges that AFM Church saved her life and kept her from going down the wrong path."

Ministries in Sri Lanka....

In recent years we have partnered with Zion Gospel Ministry in Sri Lanka, led by Prabha Subakaran. Their work is based in Colombo. Prabha says; *"My ministry's leadership is Holy Spirit. He is the owner of my ministry, according to Psalm 32:8; 'I will instruct you and teach you in the way you should go, I will counsel you and watch over you.' My ministry is to glorify the name of Jesus, the Name that is above all other Names!"*

Prabha and his team are involved locally in the following areas: Church ministry; distributing tracts; hospital ministry; healing and deliverance; fasting; outer gospel ministry; rehabilitation ministry; counselling for families; children's ministry and youth ministry.

He went on to tell me; *"Because of our friendship with Drop Inn ministries, by your guidance and teachings of the Bible, spiritually I could overcome all obstacles in my ministry. I can assure you that after friendship with Drop Inn team, brother Ronnie and his family, ministry boundaries have extended lavishly. May God's faithful love be with you and through His name your horn exalted, according to Psalm 89:24."*

Capital - Riga
Major Religion - Lutheran Roman Catholicism
                    Russian Orthodox
Official language - Latvian
Population - 1,957,200
Currency - Euro

Latvia Formerly part of the old Soviet Union, Latvia
gained independence in 1991, but it wasn't fully ratified
until 1994. Latvia lies along the shores of the Baltic Sea and
the Gulf of Riga, and it is bounded by Estonia to the north,
Russia to the east, Belarus to the southeast, and Lithuania
to the south.

111

A relatively new EU country, Latvia was hit hard during the global financial crisis of 2008, and is now considered one of the poorest nations in the European Community.

Before Soviet occupation in 1940, ethnic Latvians constituted about three-fourths of the country's population. Today they make up about three-fifths of the population, and Russians account for about one-fourth. There are small groups of Belarusians, Ukrainians, Poles, Lithuanians, and others. The official language of Latvia is Latvian; however, nearly one-third of the population speaks Russian. Smaller numbers speak Romany, the Indo-Aryan language of the Roma (Gypsies), and Yiddish, a Germanic language. The majority of Latvians adhere to Christianity: mainly Lutheranism, Roman Catholicism, and Eastern Orthodoxy. About one-fourth of Latvians consider themselves non-religious.

CHAPTER FOURTEEN

Speaking the language...

As I have already shared, Drop Inn Community Church was planted in a portable building in Richhill in 2005 with a group of people who wanted to see God transform lives, communities and nations. We were at the time aware of many Russian-speaking people in our community. We were also aware of the restrictions the language barrier placed on fully engaging with them. To help us in our outreach, we invited two friends from Belarus, Tanya and Ira, to build relationships and to offer weekly Christian services in Russian.

Ira had been using her social media platform to share about her missionary work in Northern Ireland and tell some of the stories of how God was using them. Her posts caught the attention of a guy living in Liverpool, England called Igor. He had left his home city of Daugavpils in Latvia with a similar heart to work and serve the Lord among Russian speaking communities. After connecting with Ira online, Igor came to visit us in 2008.

He began to fly over every weekend as doors opened for him to share Jesus with many people in their own language. When their girl visas were coming to an end, we prayed about Igor coming to stay and continuing to invest in the lives of Russian speaking people in our area. While living with us, Igor was given the opportunity to visit some of the Drop Inn projects in Belarus, Ukraine and Venezuela. Every village he visited, every story of hope that he heard caused him to wonder could something similar happen in his home country. As his heart increased for the towns and villages in Latvia, he spoke to Dad about the possibilities of what could be done. Over the years, I've realised if you are going to come to my dad with a dream God is stirring in you, you better be ready to go!

At the end of 2010, Igor went on a visit to Gardene in Latvia. He was able to bless the local church with food hampers so they could give them out to people in their community; he visited other places, witnessing the need while walking the ground. When he came back to Northern Ireland, he was ready to return home to *bring hope, help and healing* to many hurting people in villages throughout Latvia. Igor gathered a team around him and began a work in old people's homes, rehab centres and prison. He did a great job establishing the work of Drop Inn in Latvia. After he got married and moved to Canada, the work has continued with Gena Cepuli since 2014.

Under Gena's leadership many of the projects continue to grow. Each week Gena and his team bring food and toiletry packages to the most vulnerable families in villages across the western part of Latvia. Through this ministry, home groups have been birthed and are developing in Biksty, Zebrene, Lyda and Zirni. The number of people gathering in these places varies from eight to 30; it is beautiful to know of little kingdom outposts scattered through this part of the country in response to hearing about the love of Jesus, but also seeing it consistently demonstrated. Over the years,

Latvia has been the place we have brought teams at Christmas time to give out our shoeboxes. These are the trips that make all the work that goes into organising them worthwhile. There are joy-filled memories that children in orphanages and poor villages hold on to all year long because someone from another country came not only to give them a gift, but also to spend time with them. In the nine years of giving out shoeboxes in Latvia, we have visited more than 40 cities and villages to hand-deliver 30,000 presents.

Drop Inn started with the hope of bringing Jesus to the young people in our village in Northern Ireland, and we have not forgotten our roots. In the majority of the countries where we have projects, we have invested heavily in youth ministry. Since 2011, we have supported our team in Latvia in hosting summer camps under the theme *'One Way Jesus.'* Young people from USA, Scotland, Belarus and Northern Ireland get together to worship, pray and carry the gospel out on to the streets. We love hearing stories of how young people in Latvia have been impacted by these camps and continue to serve the Lord passionately in their churches. It also impacts the teams that we send from Northern Ireland.

One of the young men said; *"I went to Latvia at a time when my patience was being tested in all areas; but being with the guys in Latvia, seeing how young and old would come and lay burdens down at Jesus' feet; these situations let me see how others persevered through hard times."* Another said; *"Before going to Latvia, I wasn't saved. I was a full-blown drinker and had no thought of God. I had a hole in my heart that I tried to fill with drink and drugs but was never happy. During the week, while being prayed for, I let Jesus fill the void only he could fill. My life was forever changed from that day on: now I have happiness and real joy!"*

115

Gena tells me of the influence our partnership is having in his country through the ongoing work in nursing homes, disabled homes, rehab centres, families, churches, orphanages, prisons, hospitals, alongside firefighters and social workers. In reading through the gospels, seeing the good news of Jesus impacting towns and villages but also individuals, I like how Rachel Held Evans puts it; *"It's the biggest story and the smallest story all at once."*

We celebrate all that God is doing in Latvia; but we also celebrate what He is doing in Gena. He told me how Drop Inn has affected his personal life. Gena was pastoring a church in a small village believing this was his calling. He didn't have many contacts or friends around the world and had never left his country. As a result of attending our European conference, that has changed. The biggest lesson Gena has learned is to remove the limits he has placed on God. I'm not saying everyone has to leave their country or have friends around the world but I think we could all be challenged to remove the limits we have placed on what God wants to do, and maybe what He wants to do through you.

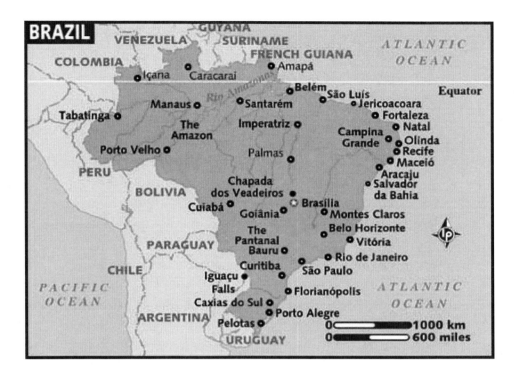

Capital - Brasília
Major religion - Roman catholicism
Official Language - Portuguese
Population - 202,768,562
Currency - real (R$ plural reais)

Brazil is the fifth most-populous country on Earth and accounts for one-third of Latin America's population. Most of the inhabitants of Brazil are concentrated along the eastern seaboard, although its capital, Brasília, is located far inland, and increasing numbers of migrants are moving to the interior. Rio de Janeiro, in the eyes of many of the world, continues to be the pre-eminent icon of Brazil.

The nation's burgeoning cities, huge hydroelectric and industrial complexes, mines, and fertile farmlands make it one of the world's major economies. However, Brazil struggles with extreme social inequalities, environmental degradation, intermittent financial crises, and sometimes a deadlocked political system.

Brazil is unique in the Americas because, following independence from Portugal, it did not fragment into separate countries as did British and Spanish possessions in the region; rather, it retained its identity through the intervening centuries and a variety of forms of government. Because of that hegemony, the Portuguese language is universal except among Brazil's native Indians, especially those in the more remote reaches of the Amazon basin. At the turn of the 21st century, Brazilians marked the 500th anniversary of Portuguese contact with a mixture of public celebration and deprecation.

CHAPTER FIFTEEN

A home for street children...

Noel Quinlan (born in Ireland) and Sandra (born in England) had served as missionaries for many years in Brazil. When they retired in 1997, they couldn't get Brazil and its children out of their minds; so along with a small group of friends, they started LAM, *Latin American Ministries*. Their heart was to see something established in over-populated slum-type urban areas. They had experienced the poverty that children and their families were living in and wanted to provide opportunities that were not available to them.

From its small beginnings, LAM was able to build two churches, establish and support four schools and two youth support centres, and also build a home for 'street children,' all in Rio de Janeiro. They built two schools to serve the native Indians and Brazilians living in the Amazon jungle area of the country. All of the children who attended these schools were from extremely poor families, most living in a one-parent situation, many severely traumatised and suffering from the violence and hunger that was their daily experience. They went with the words of Jesus in Matthew 18:14 as their motivation: *"It is not the will of your Father in heaven that one of these little ones should perish,"* (*CSB, Christian Standard Bible*)

LAM have continued to come alongside pastors and churches with a holistic approach to serving the young people in their communities by providing nourishing meals and basic skills that come with normal education; and also showing the love of God by what they say and what they do. As a result, many of the children and their families have been reached and their lives have been changed: through the message of Jesus they have been given hope beyond their situation. To be able to help the children and ministries God had put them in contact with, LAM have depended on faithful partners to help fund the different projects and schools.

Noel and Sandra met Mum and Dad through mutual friends just as they were beginning this beautiful ministry. They became good friends, and Drop Inn have been one of their main supporters ever since. In my communication with Sandra she told me; *"We are extremely grateful for the faithfulness of Drop Inn over all these years as without their very important contribution to the work, LAM would not have been able to accomplish all that has been done so far. We would like to congratulate them on their 25 years of wonderful, fruitful ministry all over the world!"*

One of the schools LAM were supporting was *The Living Word School* in Maues right in the heart of the Amazon. Noel and Sandra told us about a couple who were serving the Lord in this place. Marty Davison grew up in Belfast, studied at Queens University before going on to work as a dentist in Ballymena. Within a short period of time, God radically changed the direction and course of his life. Marty went on a trip to Brazil with his local church as their *'missionary dentist,'* and within a short period of time this dentist from Belfast was married to a beautiful Brazilian called Rebecca and living in the heart of the Amazon.

I'll let Marty share... "*I had no theological degree, no previous missionary experience, no database of supporters, and was fundamentally anonymous at the ends of the earth trying to serve God. Support was minimal, times were tough and often it felt like the light at the end of the tunnel was just another train coming to run us over. But through those days you hold onto the word; youthful zeal gets burned up and God works on you for His glory.*

"*I'd never heard of Drop Inn before, even when I was in Northern Ireland. But Ronnie and Carolyn had been out to Brazil and had met Noel and Sandra Quinlan. All of a sudden, never having been to Maues, Drop Inn Ministries was supporting the work of the school, and also Rebecca and me personally.*

"*I was amazed! We hadn't actually met these people, but they were supporting us. Drop Inn was an answer to prayer; our first regular support from any church or organisation. Before long, teams were coming to the Amazon from Drop Inn. These teams are fantastic, the vibrancy and energy that they bring, the willingness of heart and servanthood. They live out their motto, 'bringing hope, help and healing to a hurting world.' We found what was written on the tin was exactly what was inside, always refreshing.*"

Our team trips to Brazil, in particular to Maues, were the most extraordinary experiences for many that were involved. We would spend a few days in Rio de Janeiro visiting the incredible projects LAM were running in some of the slum areas of the city. We also got to visit some of the stunning sites, including Sugar Loaf Mountain and the 'Christ the Redeemer' statue.

The adventure would continue when we took a four-hour flight from Rio to Manaus. We bought a hammock there, which became our bed for the overnight riverboat journey down the Amazon River. Every time our little boat docked in Maues, almost 24 hours later, we were greeted enthusiastically by Marty and his family. On every visit we had the opportunity to serve the school, to encourage the church and respond to needs as we spent time with people in the community.

Again, Marty continues... *"There are many, many stories to be told from all the teams that came out, too many to recount, yet each one had the same underlying qualities: great workers, willing to muck in, with much laughter. I remember we went out delivering food hampers to some of the families whose children attended the Living Word School. Because of Drop Inn's support, the children were fed well at school, clothed in uniform, and teachers received gifts for their hard work. So the children 'looked' lovely in school; but to see their reality was a must.*

"This particular day it was pouring with rain, I suppose that's why they call the Amazon a rainforest. Standing in this little shack, we presented the hamper to the mother and prayed with her. There was more rain coming in through the palm leaf roof than outside. The team wanted to do something; they couldn't see such a need and not respond. The next day we were back again, this time with wood for rafters and roof tiles. Within a short period of time, the family literally had a new roof over their heads!"

Throughout the story of Drop Inn, I hope the value we place on relationships and family has been evident. Marty's closing thoughts are another reminder...

"Drop Inn Ministries became family: they had adopted us and we them! For us it has been a pleasure to watch the ministry grow as God has blessed them. It is no surprise that the ministry continues to grow as the core values continue to be passed from one generation to the other: their love, their Kingdom values, integrity, faithfulness, laughter and family, with God at the centre of it all."

Transforming Venezuela...

Partnering with others to see their vision come to life has been really exciting. In 2006, Mum and Dad met Nigel Burrows, originally from Dungannon but with a big dream to see Venezuela transformed with the good news of Jesus. Back in 2002, Nigel had attended a one-year programme with YWAM in Denver, Colorado, and it was during that year he made his first visit to Venezuela. He was part of a team of 18 from the YWAM base who went to serve in Barquisimeto, one of Venezuela's biggest cities.

It turned out to be a life-changing experience for Nigel. As an evangelist, he was amazed at how open people were to the Word of God; but equally, he was devastated to see so much need in the slums they were working into. In February 2003, he returned to Venezuela alongside a ministry from Mississippi, USA, with a one-year commitment to continue to serve the people of Barquisimeto. By 2004, Nigel had decided to stay on and focus his attention on evangelising to this city of two million people spread out over an area of 100 square miles.

The vision God gave him was a map of the city and the strategy of marking off every street with a pen, as he knocked on every door and shared Jesus in some way with all that he met. He bought himself a map, but he had no team, no Spanish language, no finances and no written materials. Even though it sounded crazy, he was convinced God was guiding his steps. Gradually a team began to gather round him.

There isn't enough space to share the stories of how they saw God do the most amazing things as they worked across the city. They worked their way from the south-east corner to the north-west corner. It took eight years to complete and over this time they were able to give 440,000 pieces of Christian literature that shared the love of Jesus and saw around 5,000 decisions being made to follow Him.

It was just a year into this project that Nigel began crying out to God for two things: firstly, a home church in Northern Ireland; and secondly, help to provide for the many poor families he had been meeting in the slums. There were so many times that he was invited into the homes of these people and on experiencing the conditions in which they were trying to survive, he became desperate to find some help to give. He also wanted to offer some hope and to see healing through the gospel come into their lives. He had learned in his time with YWAM that 'knowledge = responsibility.'

In a roundabout way, Nigel was put in contact with Drop Inn by accident. During his time in Venezuela, he had to leave the country every three months to renew his visa, so he had been on mission trips into Trinidad and Tobago many times and had built a good relationship with Dr Brian Lushington, who ran a mission organisation in the country. The first time Nigel planned to visit Trinidad and Tobago, he got in touch with a missions organisation who gladly offered him accommodation for a couple of nights during his stay. When he got to the airport in Port of Spain, the capital city, after collecting his baggage he was greeted by a young man who asked if he was *the missionary?*

Nigel said that he was. The young man led him to the car where he was introduced to Dr Brian. About 30 minutes into their journey, as they were sharing their mission experiences, Dr Brian received a call from another pastor who was also waiting at the airport for a missionary! Nigel had been picked up by the wrong person, but listened in to their conversation as they decided that *'if you are happy with your missionary, I'm happy with mine!'* We have realised over the years that what seems accidental is not always accidental. Maybe God is teaching us that He has a way of correcting the course.

From the first conversation Nigel had with Dr Brian, he was asked did he know a man in Northern Ireland called Philip Proctor; and every time Nigel told him he didn't. After a couple of years, Dr Brian insisted that Nigel make contact with Philip the next time he was back home in Northern Ireland. In early 2006, when Nigel was home, he met Philip for coffee and had a great time of fellowship as he shared some of the highs and lows of being on the mission field. He shared the frustrations that he had experienced working with some of the poorest people in the slums of Barquisimeto, and how he had a deep desire to find a way of bringing help to these people. Philip told Nigel about a man he knew in Richhill called Ronnie Dawson. Philip got in touch with Dad and arranged for him and Nigel to meet and 25 minutes later Nigel met my parents in our charity shop at Stonebridge just outside Richhill.

They shared stories, shared their hearts, and shared a conviction that the gospel as Jesus revealed was a holistic gospel covering not

125

just the spiritual needs, but meeting other areas of human need too. Nigel asked if Drop Inn were able to send a container of humanitarian aid to Venezuela. Dad told Nigel the cost of sending a container would be £6,000, told him the length of time it would take to get there, not to mention all the other logistics. However, in his next breath, Dad asked if giving him £500 a month over the next year would be a better solution? Nigel was amazed that someone he had just met was willing to make such a commitment. Yet for Dad he was so moved by his desire to bring help to people living in desperate need that he was willing to encourage him financially. Soon after, we began to encourage and support Nigel and the team practically. We took many teams into Venezuela; one trip in 2009 included my three-month old son!

Since 2006, support from Drop Inn has meant many families in the slum areas have received regular food parcels. We were able to open a feeding centre at the church in the area, pastored by a wonderful man called Diego. Every week between 120 and 150 kids get a hot nutritious meal. We have also had the joy of supporting local pastors and the 'Light of Hope' orphanage. In 2015, Nigel left Venezuela to establish the work we were undertaking in Greece. The evangelism and programmes continue under the leadership of a local lady called Desirée.

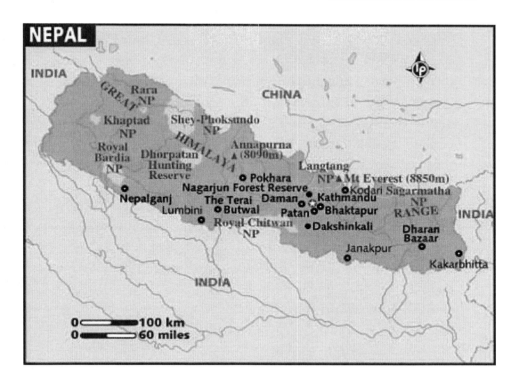

Capital - Kathmandu
Major Religion - Hinduism
Official Language - Nepali
Population - 26,494,504
Currency - Nepalese Rupee

Nepal is a country of Asia, lying along the southern slopes of the Himalayan mountain ranges. It is a landlocked country located between India to the east, south, and west and the Tibet Autonomous Region of China to the north. Its territory extends roughly 500 miles (800 kilometres) from east to west and 90 to 150 miles from north to south. The capital is Kathmandu.

Wedged between two giants, India and China, Nepal seeks to keep a balance between the two countries in its foreign policy, and thus to remain independent. A factor that contributes immensely to the geopolitical importance of the country is the fact that a strong Nepal can deny China access to the rich Gangetic Plain; Nepal thus marks the southern boundary of the Chinese sphere north of the Himalayas in Asia.

Disaster struck when a devastating earthquake hit Nepal on 25th April 2015, killing approximately 9,000 people. Hundreds of thousands of people were rendered homeless. People were literally sleeping on the roadsides in shelters made of plastics and tarpaulin.

In Nepal a vast majority of the population is Hindu, but a small percentage follows Buddhism or other religious faiths. Hindus and Buddhists tend to be concentrated in areas where Indian and Tibetan cultural influences, respectively, have been dominant.

CHAPTER SIXTEEN

Natural disasters...

In the same way that Drop Inn started in response to an obvious need in 1994, it has become our habit to respond to situations of crisis around the world. It is difficult when you have seen devastation of lives and livelihoods to *un-see* it. It is even harder to ignore it once you have heard a cry for help.

A devastating earthquake struck Nepal on 25th April 2015, killing almost 7,000 people. It was followed by many aftershocks that went on damaging buildings and houses, and destroying lives. This was one of those times where we were able to jump into immediate action. We sent a team from Northern Ireland that was led by our contact on the ground, Reuben, to join local church leaders. They first went to a village in Sindhupalchouk district, the epicentre of the earthquake, to distribute food, clothing and medicines in an area where most of the old houses were destroyed and people were living in makeshift tents. We did the same thing in another place at the heart of Kathmandu, the nation's capital city, where people were living in about 200 tents spread in an open field called Ratna Park. These tents were 10ft x 12ft, with about 20 people (4/5 families) cramped into each one of them.

After some months, the authorities began asking people to go back to the places they had come from. The tents began to get dismantled. However, there were two tents left because the people simply had nowhere to go. With increasing pressure on these families to vacate their tents, once again there was an immediate response for us to make, so we leased a plot of land in the suburbs with a contract of five years and constructed shelters for ten families. As the need was urgent, houses were initially made of a temporary nature, with bamboo used as frameworks and corrugated tin for the sides and roof. Plain mud was the floor. Alongside this support, we helped a few families start small businesses so they could rebuild their livelihoods.

Reuben, who was now living in India, oversaw the work and the needs of the people in this camp, with the help of a local pastor called Robinson. Unfortunately, after two years the bamboo frames were creaking, the roofs were leaking and rats were making holes in the floor. Once again, we began to raise funds. We asked our shop managers to put up posters in our shops asking the public to 'buy a brick and build a home.' It wasn't long before we had gathered enough to renovate the whole camp and built a more solid structure. This time, construction was done by installing iron rods as the framework. The floor was cemented and the heights of the roof were raised for better ventilation and space. These ten houses for ten families still stand strong today!

The people are still standing strong, too. Today, almost all in the camp are Believers, with a significant number of them being baptised and part of the local church. Some of the people, particularly those who started their own little businesses, who were there at the beginning, have moved on; but the camp is able to provide shelter for others who find themselves in a dire situation and need immediate shelter.

Interestingly, the army people who were stationed in Ratna Park to look after the 200 tents, who had to continue to be there for the sake of the last two tents, became familiar with Drop Inn and its people. In their log book, Drop Inn was registered. They were so pleased when we told them we had built a shelter for people living in those last two tents.

Haiti...

After spending some time with Pastor Lesley in Haiti in 2005 and with our friend Eugene Smith, we began investing in the building they had for young boys and girls who had been orphaned. More important than that, we invested in the children, meeting their basic needs, food, clothes and education. It has also been our joy to invest in local pastors, in their commitment to seeing churches planted in their nation.

It was late afternoon on 12th January 2010 when a magnitude 7.0 earthquake struck Haiti. In a country that had been suffering years of political, social, and economic turmoil, this disaster left the people of Haiti facing their greatest humanitarian need yet. It was estimated that three million people were affected by the devastation that was caused. Upwards of 150,000 lost their lives with many more injured. Almost 4,000 schools were damaged or destroyed along with many homes and businesses. Once again the statistics were overwhelming, the need was massive but, just as we would, years later, in Nepal and Greece, we responded immediately.

We were able to send a team of workmen along with finances to support our friends who had lost everything. In a way, it felt like the young boy in a crowd of over 5,000 people offering his meagre five loaves and two fish. We all need reminding that whatever is in our hand, no matter how small, something happens when we offer it to Jesus. One of the main things we took responsibility for was the rebuilding of the orphanage wall that had collapsed. These kids had already experienced dreadful loss and devastation in their young lives, so, in their time of extreme vulnerability, we wanted to do what we could to make them feel as safe as possible. Our team from Northern Ireland completed the project in conditions they were certainly not accustomed to, working long days in 40-degree heat, with no air conditioning.

The consequences of this earthquake are still being felt today. It is one of the places for which we need to find more sponsors. Fewer kids are being educated because of poverty and the destruction of school buildings. We need people who will help to give young children in Haiti the chance to go to school but also to help older kids who need a way back in. On a recent team visit to Haiti, David spoke with young boys who still have hopes and ambitions, but need people to sponsor their education to help see their dreams become reality. If you would like to help with our child sponsorship programme, please see the back of the book for further details.

CHAPTER SEVENTEEN

A call to action...

Our response to the earthquakes in Haiti and Nepal were immediate, so when the global refugee crisis began to make headlines, we once again rallied a team of people and gathered whatever finances were available to send to Athens, Greece.

In 2015, because of the terror of war and threat on life, the number of refugees fleeing their homes had dramatically increased. There were huge amounts of people crossing the waters. The risks of such a crossing were high; but such was the fear, families were left feeling there was no other option for them. It was on 1st September 2015 that this crisis caught the attention of the world, with many media outlets releasing the image of a little boy's body washed up on a Turkish beach. Alan Kurdi was only three-years-old and, along with his family, was fleeing from the war in Syria. It was this heart-wrenching image that was the catalyst for many to pray and to give and for some to go.

It was five days later, on 6th September that Drop Inn had a team on the ground to see how we could serve this massive gathering of people. On this first trip, the team spent much of their time in Victoria Square in the centre of Athens, where thousands had gathered. It was another one of those occasions when the need seemed overwhelming. Our team met many vulnerable, grieving families, who had experienced loss of family members in their attempt to find safety. They met young people on their own who needed water and something to eat. There were times when they didn't know what to say or what to do as they engaged with so many difficult stories. Yet they knew they could pray and they could worship Jesus, so they did that.

These are the times when like King Jehoshaphat, we pray that same prayer; *"Oh God…we don't know what to do but our eyes are on you."* (2 Chronicles 20:12) In this biblical story, Jehoshaphat's plan to take on the battle he was faced with seems strange. He sent out the worshippers at the front line of battle and declared that the love of God endures forever! (v21) The team tried this same tactic.

In March 2016, when Macedonia decided to close their borders, it left tens of thousands of refugees stranded in Greece. Nigel Burrows led a team to the Macedonian border, to a small village where 10,000 people were struggling. The team gave out food and clothes to many families who queued for hours to make sure their children were fed and kept warm. During our visits we were working with and building relationships with many Iranian, Afghan and Syrian families. In our times of prayer together, we were asking God if there was more we should do.

We felt an increasing responsibility towards those we had been partnering with and those we were helping, so Nigel became our full-time representative in Athens. He went with a one-year commitment, with the intention of coming alongside established NGO's as well as the local church and a newly-established Iranian fellowship. Our base in the city not only kept us central to all that was going on, it meant we were able to bring teams in from different churches locally, and other connections globally, who were equally passionate about responding to this crisis.

I hope throughout our story you have seen our commitment to the 'ones.' There are many individuals we have met who are so much more than just another statistic. Every person we have encountered along the way has one thing in common, with each other and with us: all are made in the image of God, who places significant value and worth on each one.

It was in the early days of setting up base that Nigel met Bashir, (not real name) he was a Christian man from Iran but had fled his country because of persecution. Bashir ended up on the streets of Athens addicted to prescription drugs. Nigel did what he could to help him but often would find him lying helplessly in his own vomit. There were times Nigel wondered whether he would survive another winter. Nigel refused to give up on him. Then Bashir found out he had a brain tumour. After a successful operation, he spent three months in hospital. Nigel lived out the challenge of Jesus; 'I was sick and you looked after me.' Matthew 25:36. It was at this time that Bashir got clean from his addiction and is now living in a halfway house in a different part of the country. He is walking close to Jesus: he has been set free!

We came across many other nationalities during our time in Greece. The devastation of war and poverty was the reason we met people from Libya, Morocco and Tunisia. There were almost 700 we were able to help with food, tents and boots. As the boots were handed out, I become so aware that I will never walk in what these families have walked in. Too often our default position towards people we don't understand is one of judgement. We are told stories that can cause us to dehumanise people. There is a famous saying: *'Before you judge a man, walk a mile in his shoes.'*

As we listen to the stories these courageous people have to tell, I've tried to put lessons learned into practice, no matter where I am or who I find myself with. I especially remember the advice; *'Be quick to listen and slow to speak.'* My intention is that before passing judgement, I would understand their experiences, their challenges and mindset.

Impacting Turkey...

I have already introduced you to Sasha. He had been in rehab but is now pastoring a church that is overseeing the development of rehab centres in Belarus and also among our partners in Eastern Europe. Sasha and his wife had gone with Mum and Dad and two other couples to Turkey to pray for the Middle East and discern the next steps towards serving the Lord and His people in this part of the world. On this trip they were staying in the home of friends of Mum and Dad's in Dalaman, on the south-eastern coast of Turkey. On the first day of this prayer retreat they talked about how good it would be to connect with a church in Turkey and prayed that God would open a door to make that possible.

One of the men from Belarus posted on his Facebook page, saying where they were and what they were praying for. The next day one of his 'friends' living in Norway sent them a phone number of a man leading a church in a place called Fethiye which was 44km away. Dad called the number, and the following day was having lunch with Paul Hembrough, sharing their stories of what God had been doing in their lives up until this point. Paul and his wife Lynda had left the comforts of their home in England to set up a ministry in Turkey called *turksworks*.

They began this work because of the injustice they witnessed, especially with employment and knew they could not stand back and do nothing. This is a couple whose hearts are for the lost, the poor, the broken and forgotten, so they began to do what they could to reach out to people and see their circumstances and their lives change. Paul told me; *"God loves justice and mercy and we soon discovered Drop Inn do too! They offered to partner with us to help reach more people and see more lives changed one at a time, which is typical of the heart of Drop Inn. It is this love for people and how that moves them into action that is so admirable, and a true mark of Ronnie and Carolyn's walk with God and their love for Him."*

Psalm 41:1-3 are key verses that Paul and Lynda hold on to in their daily service: *"Oh, the joys of those who are kind to the poor! The Lord rescues them when they are in trouble. The Lord protects them and keeps them alive. He gives them prosperity in the land and rescues them from their enemies. The Lord nurses them when they are sick and restores them to health."*

We recognise they are truly on the front-line of Kingdom ministry, owing to the nature of what Paul and Lynda are called to do and the nature of the place they are called to do it. Turkey is 99.8% Muslim with a Protestant church numbering around 7,000 in a population of 80 million. There are more mosques per capita in Turkey than any other nation in the world and more Imams than teachers or doctors. Every child is taught that to be a Turk is to be a Muslim and as they are so proud of their country, for most Turks' it is unthinkable to be anything other than Muslim. Christian leaders (foreigners) are being evicted or refused re-entry into Turkey at an increasing rate, even as we write this book.

Paul recently received an email which he shared with me...

'In recent months, about twenty brothers have been prevented from entering the country. And in total about fifty or more since last year. Today, another two more! Times are changing, and the darkness closes in; so how vital it is for the light of Christ to shine ever more brightly in those who are known by His name!'

One of our deepest prayers for Paul and Lynda and others who work alongside us is that they would be able to lay down what can so often feel heavy. Jesus invites those that are weary and carrying heavy burdens to come to Him for rest. We hope to create an environment where people will take Jesus' yoke upon them and find rest for their souls; because His yoke is easy and His burden is light. I love how Eugene Peterson translates these words of Jesus in Matthew 11:28-30; *'Are you tired? Worn out? Burned out on religion? Come to me. Get away with me and you'll recover your life. I'll show you how to take a real rest. Walk with me and work with me, watch how I do it. Learn the unforced rhythms of grace. I won't lay anything heavy or ill-fitting on you. Keep company with me and you'll learn to live freely and lightly.'*

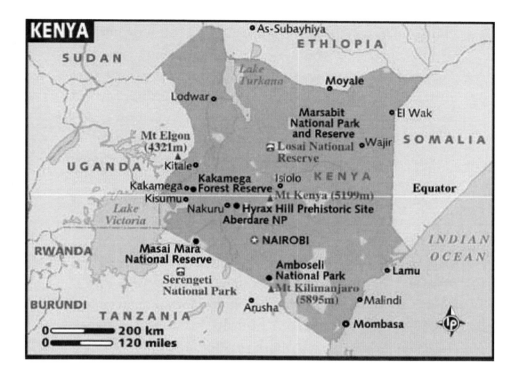

Capital - Nairobi
Major religion -
Official Language - Kiswahili
Population - 45,010,056
Currency - Kenyan shilling

Kenya is a country in East Africa famed for its scenic landscapes and vast wildlife preserves. Its Indian Ocean coast provided historically important ports by which goods from Arabian and Asian traders have entered the continent for many centuries. Along that coast, which holds some of the finest beaches in Africa, are predominantly Muslim Swahili cities such as Mombasa, a historic centre that has contributed much to the musical and culinary heritage of the country. Inland are populous highlands famed for both their tea plantations, an economic staple during the British colonial era, and their variety of animal species, including lions, elephants, cheetahs, rhinoceroses, and hippopotamuses. Kenya's western provinces, marked by lakes and rivers, are forested, while a small portion of the north is desert and semi-desert. The country's diverse wildlife and panoramic geography draw large numbers of European and North American visitors, and tourism is an important contributor to Kenya's economy.

Freedom of religion is guaranteed by the constitution. More than four-fifths of the people are Christian, primarily attending Protestant or Roman Catholic churches. Christianity first came to Kenya in the 15th century through the Portuguese, but this contact ended in the 17th century. Christianity was revived at the end of the 19th century and expanded rapidly. African traditional religions have a concept of a supreme being who is known by various names. Many syncretic faiths have arisen in which the adherents borrow from Christian traditions and African religious practices. Independent churches are numerous; one such church, the Maria Legio of Africa, is dominated by the Luo people. Muslims constitute a sizeable minority and include both Sunnis and Shī'ites. There are also small populations of Jews, Jains, Sikhs, and Baha'is. In remote areas, Christian mission stations offer educational and medical facilities as well as religious ones.

CHAPTER EIGHTEEN

A drop in the ocean...

In 2009, my brother-in-law David McBride (I will share more about him later) was studying at Belfast Bible College.

In his small group he got to know Dr Paul Mwangi, from Kenya. Paul had come for a three-month course at the college. During his stay he received news that he would have no employment when he returned home. This was a devastating blow to Paul and his family and also to his desire to help families in the slum areas of his city. Before he left for home, David wanted to bring Paul to spend some time with Dad. It was clear that this humble follower of Jesus had no other motivation but to live and serve the most needy and the too-often neglected in one of the most difficult places to live in Nairobi. We made an initial commitment to supporting Paul personally, and to create a food programme for ten families in the Mukuru slum. Mukuru is one of the largest slums in Nairobi. It stretches along the Ngong river, situated in wastelands in the industrial area of the city. More than 100,000 people live inside.

If there was enough money left over after filling the food hampers, Paul would buy crafts for the women living in the community. These incredible women are so creative and were able to make products that could be sold at the local market. We used an increased income to increase the number of families we could support.

It was 2012 when David and I were sent to visit Paul in Kenya and meet the families and projects he was overseeing. It is easy to feel overwhelmed when the need is so big and your contribution feels like a drop in the ocean. At these times I try and remind myself of a well-known story...

An old man was walking along the beach one morning. A big storm had recently passed and the beach was littered with starfish as far as he could see. In the distance the old man saw a young boy throwing a starfish back into the sea. The old man questioned the boy saying; *"There must be tens of thousands of starfish on this beach. I'm afraid you won't really be able to make much of a difference."* The boy's response was to bend down, pick up another starfish, throw it into the ocean and smiling at the old man he said; *"It made a difference to that one!"*

In Mukuru slum, we met whole families living in tiny one-room corrugated iron shacks, about 3m x 3m. Very few homes had any power. Up to 20 families shared a toilet and water tap. This massive slum area filled with tens of thousands of little shacks. In the first shack we visited was a woman who had been diagnosed with HIV. Her husband had left her and she was bringing up her two children on her own. She had started to make handbags out of plastic bags to sell at the market which had given her a sense of purpose. She told us the difference our support was making to her family.

These experiences are why we place such high value on bringing people to visit our projects around the world. Sitting face to face with someone, making the need personal has a real impact on those that are visiting and on those who are being visited. Whatever the scale, of what we do, we want to do it the best we can. As much as anything else, we want people to know the value and worth that God has placed on them.

Making a difference with coffee…

At the start of 2013, we got a phone call from a friend who was running a coffee shop in our local town, Portadown. He was planning to close it down but wanted to ask us first if we were interested in taking it on. Our initial response was that we knew nothing about how to run a coffee shop but we would pray about it just in case God wanted to say something different!

With Kenya still on our minds, David and I began to dream together. On a work trip to Dublin, where we had time to talk, we wondered could we create an environment that would visually represent the place we would then support by selling coffee. It was one of those unique occasions that by the time we got home, we had a plan of what we were going to try, how it was going to look, what it was going to be called and we even had the logo! We bought corrugated iron for the walls; we recycled old doors as tables and pallets as seating, and opened the shop: *Tin House Coffee*. We put pictures up of the slum area we visited, to increase our support of this new venture. We still didn't know how to run a coffee shop; but we learned lessons along the way. We were so grateful for a community that supported us, knowing that buying a coffee was helping make a difference in the lives of families in Kenya.

After a couple of years, it became clear we needed a bigger place. We had been praying for months that somewhere would become clear for us to move to. One day in the summer of 2016, we were offered a large building in the centre of Portadown; and they needed a decision by that Friday. We kept praying and thinking it was too big, we couldn't settle on what to do, right up to the deadline. On the Friday, Mum and Dad, David and Nicola, Judith and I were visiting friends for dinner.

I got a phone call from a good friend of ours, David Spence, who wanted to tell me about a dream he had the night before. He knew nothing about our thoughts or plans to move; but in his dream, Tin House was in a building three times the current size, there was live music and he got the words of Isaiah 54; *'Clear lots of ground for your tents, make your tents large, spread out, think big!'* It was a beautiful moment to receive this confirmation when we were all together as a family. A few months later, Tin House Coffee moved into a three-storey building. The space continues to be used for live music and various community events.

A contribution from Kenya…

As previously mentioned, Dr Paul Mwangi from Kenya became a good friend of ours, he wanted to share his story. This is what he said…

"*After the visit of Ronnie to Belfast Bible College, we continued to meet and share with David on the way forward. By the time we were parting ways at the end of the training, I had a clear mind on starting a feeding programme and building it as part of the Drop Inn Ministry in Kenya. The meeting and the training at Belfast Bible College was such a blessing into my ministry. Back in Kenya, I shared my experience with my fellow local church leaders of Africa Inland Church Riruta, an evangelical church committed to the holistic ministry.*

"*The church is located in a place called Kawangware, it is one of the peri-urban (slums) areas in north-west of Nairobi town. The majority of the people who are within a 15 kilometre circumference are families of meagre means (less than a dollar a day) of livelihood. In this regard, malnutrition, joblessness and crime levels are very high.*

"*It is the desire of AIC Riruta to be involved in holistic ministry to the community and, more so, to the members who worship with us. From the onset and on the basis of my ministerial formation, I desired to have programmes that would minister holistically to the needs of the members and the community that is within our catchment area. The ministry would move in phases, starting with the feeding programme that addressed malnutrition in some of the peri-urban households. Other programmes would be initiated as time goes on. Each programme has the following components: Physical – food, clothing, shelter. Spiritual – Discipleship. Social – Growing with others.*

"*When the needy cases were identified, we bought foodstuffs on a monthly basis for ten households. While delivering the food, moments for prayer and Bible study were observed. We believed that at the heart of the ministry is the proclamation of the love of God to the hurting in the community. After the blessings from the church leadership to initiate the feeding programme, I laid a foundation for the Drop Inn Ministry Kenyan chapter. I had identified vulnerable families through the Sunday school teachers.*

"In late August 2010 we received the first support of £300.00 that went to the feeding programme. The money catered for the basic foods to families that were surviving on less than £1.00 per day. From May 2011, we added two more households. One was a widow with her four children. The husband and the father of her children died in a very tragic car accident in the month of April 2011. The other household had three children whose parents were living on less than a pound per day.

"The support has been very significant for all the households. The children who used to go to school without breakfast, and other times sleeping without a meal, saw the love of God in the Drop Inn Ministry feeding programme. For sure there was help, hope and healing all by the grace of God. The mothers of the children were very enthusiastic about the support they received.

"Today the families do not have the burden of raising young children with a budget of less than a pound per day. They look back and praise God for the support that Drop Inn Ministries accorded them. The children are now grown up and some have their families. Above all, they are stable financially and serving God.

"By late 2012, my wife Mary and I decided to add skills to the rations as we expand the ministry. The beneficiaries received the skill training very well. We started by training 20 households in Kawangware. These are households who have been earning less than a pound a day. In time they will be earning close to four pounds a day or even more.

"*Every household was receiving on average five pounds every Saturday from the sale of the handcrafts. The households welcomed the initiative with much thanks. With time, the skill will make a family that had no livelihood to have hope to see a new day with thankfulness to God for a chance to have something to do and have food security. The handcraft programme grew to a point of supplementing the budgets of about 30 households in three peri-urban areas. This meant that we changed the strategy from monthly rations to daily activities that keep the guardians actively busy preparing handcrafts (flowers) that are used in the Maasai Sandals.*

"*All in all, we have come to learn that there are many adults who are parents who don't have anything constructive to do with their lives on a daily basis. Drop Inn Ministries Kenya is filling the gap with a place to meet (church) and something to do (skills) and at the end of the week they get £6 to £10. The women were appreciative of the hope and help that Drop Inn Ministries gives to them as mothers. For sure, to God be the glory!*

"*With Mary's help, the women formed what Kenyans call Chamaa (merry-go-round group) where every Friday each contributes to a common fund, which is then shared by two members. The sharing rotates until each member has received the chamaa. Using the chamaa money the women are in a position to increase their purchasing power.*

"*Other forms of ministry we have been involved in include leadership training for women and other church groups. We are grateful to God for the love he has lavished upon us and we continue to appreciate the paths of service through Drop Inn Ministries.*

"By and large, help, healing and hope are the main virtues for Drop Inn Ministries. We have endeavoured to serve human beings without distinction and whatever their need. It has been a compassionate task to aid the vulnerable and the victims of drought and famine and to help set up development schemes, literacy campaigns, and health education.

"We have a particular responsibility to minister to the needs of the handicapped, old people, the bereaved, children at risk and families in tension, and to rehabilitate offenders against the law, alcoholics, drug-addicts and chronic gamblers."

CHAPTER NINETEEN

The United States of America...

"Core values continue to be passed from one generation to another," is the language Marty used earlier to speak of Drop Inn.

For my sister and me, our lives have been caught up in this story from its beginning in 1994. We have seen the sacrifices, witnessed the pain at times; but also experienced the joy of all that God has done. My sister, Nicola got married to David McBride on 5th December 2007. David's ability to hear from the Father and respond to where He is already at work has opened other doors for Drop Inn in different parts of the world.

Back in 2005, David spent a year in Iowa Wesleyan University studying business. During his time there, he played for the local rugby team in Cedar Rapids. Four years later, out of the blue, David began to think about the area again. It was constantly on his heart. After waking up from a dream about Cedar Rapids at 3am on a dark February morning in 2010, he started asking God, *'why?'* David continued asking Him; *'Is there something you want me to do?'*

David went on mission teams to Haiti in July 2010 and the following month to Venezuela; but his feelings for Cedar Rapids were still as strong. As he continued to journal all the questions, all the challenges and all the opportunities that were stirring in him at this time, he did two important things that have become a habit for many of us within the Drop Inn family. Firstly, we spend time patiently seeking the Lord for discernment, for His voice; and secondly, we share what is going on with trusted friends, allowing for community discernment.

While in Venezuela, David spoke to Nigel, who knew what it was like to have a particular place so heavy on your heart. He simply advised David that he should get his feet on the ground and see if things became any clearer. Determined that is what he would do, he just had to consider how he would be able to pay his way there. On his way home from Venezuela, looking forward to seeing Nicola and their wee boy Daniel, his flight was cancelled. The airline put David up in a hotel and gave him a $400 flight voucher as compensation.

It was one day towards the end of August, after pulling out of his local petrol station, that David began to weep over Cedar Rapids and knew he had to book his flight now. This happened around the date of his birthday, so he decided the money he got from his family would go toward his trip. His birthday money plus the $400 voucher was the exact price of his flights to get him to Iowa. His plan was to go for one week and see what doors God would open. After contacting some churches in the area, he was getting discouraged when no one would take his call. This changed when he got through to Pastor Daniel Winn from Cedar Rapids Family Church, who listened to David's crazy story and said he would love to meet him. On 7th October, David met Daniel for the first time: immediately there was a genuine heart connection. This was evidenced when Daniel asked David to speak at his church that coming Sunday. This day is marked in David's memory, because after he'd finished sharing his journey of following Jesus, Daniel closed by asking people to respond: 14 people made a decision to follow Jesus too.

As he was leaving the church building that morning, David was handed a pre-paid debit card, which increased further his sense he was in the right place, at the right time. Its owner wanted to bless David with whatever was left on it, thinking there was maybe only $30 left. There was $260 to be spent, the exact amount David needed to pay for the rest of his trip.

Being led into the unknown can be a vulnerable experience. We are conditioned to hold back until we know more or until we have more. Like many of the characters in the Bible, we too are invited to trust Him in the midst of uncertainty; to be faithful with the little we do have. I am challenged by the story Jesus tells of the servants (in Matthew 25) stewarding their talents. The guy that was given one talent decided to bury what had been entrusted to him. Eugene Peterson's paraphrase of verse 25 gives us an insight into the servants mindset; *"I was afraid I might disappoint you, so I did nothing."* The following verse tells us the masters response; *"It's criminal to live cautiously like that. (v26 MSG)* I would never want that to be said of us.

Not long after David returned home, still thinking; *'why?'* Still asking; *'what now?''* Daniel sent him an email to say he was glad he took David's call that day, and went on to say that God had put him on their hearts in a most unexplainable way. Daniel was soon sharing his burden to increase the church involvement in overseas mission and started a conversation about the possibility of opening a charity shop in Cedar Rapids.

There is more of David's journaling that I could share, but it's enough to say that, in March 2012, David, Nicola and their two young boys Daniel and Joshua, made their way to Cedar Rapids, Iowa. Here David would take on the role of young adults' pastor in Cedar Rapids Family Church, while establishing Drop Inn as a charity in the USA. On 6th June 2012, Drop Inn thrift store opened in Westdale Mall in Cedar Rapids and it wasn't too long before a second shop also opened.

One of the 'why's' David asked in the midst of processing what God was birthing in him, was: why USA? Why not Asia? Why not Africa? This is where the need appears greater! He felt God say he would be used to stir a passion among people in the USA that would impact Asia and Africa.

Friendships have developed with many other churches. It is so exciting for us that, to date, there have been over 70 people from those friendships that have been on an overseas mission trip. Five of the young people from the USA have been on our one-year intern programme, all having the opportunity to encourage our brothers and sisters in India and Burkina Faso, being a blessing in Asia and Africa. At the time of writing, David, Nicola and their four kids are back living in Northern Ireland, with David overseeing the work of the charity shops here, but also keeping momentum going in the USA.

A contribution from Daniel…

My name is Daniel Winn. I met David McBride for breakfast at IHOP in Cedar Rapids, Iowa, in October of 2010. He was on a trip from Northern Ireland to investigate why God was leading him to come back to Iowa after spending a year there for his international studies. Over nine years later we can look back to see the many great things that have taken place because he responded to that nudge from the Holy Spirit.

First of all, it's been a huge blessing to have Drop Inn Iowa in existence now for over seven years. Through our partnership we have established two very successful stores, sent dozens of people on Drop Inn mission trips, had several young people participate in the Drop Inn gap year programme, and partnered financially with the Burkina Faso project to see our donations build a much-needed medical clinic in the city of Koudougou.

However, by far the most amazing piece of this partnership has been the relationships that have been established. Us Iowans have been so privileged to become friends with some of the most amazing people from all over the world that are part of the Drop Inn family. Because of those relationships, we have seen the Kingdom of God expand through people in ways that only God can make possible.

To this day we continue to be inspired by these individuals' faith. We're strengthened by their testimonies, and we're encouraged by their love. My own personal family has been richly blessed through the warmth and friendship of the Drop Inn family.

All of this began because someone listened and responded to what seemed right to them and the Holy Spirit. It seems that this captures what Drop Inn has been about for all these years...praying, listening, and responding to the Holy Spirit.

CHAPTER TWENTY

The keys of the castle...

We had been referring some of the people we were working with locally to the Stauros foundation, who at that time were based at Ballyards castle. Little did we know then, but this remarkable building would become very significant for us in our own journey.

The land on which Ballyards stands was purchased in 1713 by the Simpson family. The family prospered in the area around the late seventeen hundreds. There is a record of military achievements in the Royal Irish Fusiliers, and also as magistrates in the local area. The family used the water power of the Callen River, deriving their substantial fortune from linen. Linen was laid out to bleach in the fields around Ballyards. The Simpson family are associated with many local grand properties, including Linen Hill House and Beech Hill House. In the 1860's, Colonel Thomas Simpson constructed the modern building of Ballyards House. He completed it in 1872, although it is thought that he never actually lived in it by the time he died in 1892. His widow continued to live here until she sold Ballyards in 1908.

In addition to the feature of a tower, Ballyards was built with a conservatory and veranda, both of which are now gone, and the building cost then in the region of £3,600. The coat of arms found on the skylight in the main entrance hall belongs to the Simpsons. It translates as 'King, Kingdom, Faithful,' a motto that is still practised today; but to a different King and Kingdom.

The next owner was a local flax miller, Maynard Sinton. He added to the original building; by 1916 there was the oak room extension onto the rear of the house, the nursery and servant quarters in the north-east wing; also the addition of servant quarters and the north-west wing. This almost doubled the size of the original building. It was during this period that the name was changed to Ballyards Castle. After the 2nd World War, Ballyards was occupied by different organisations but then lay dormant for years. In a remarkable act of faith, the castle was bought by the Paynter family, who were local to the area, to be used for Christian work.

The Stauros foundation were the first to benefit from this radical act of generosity. Stauros is a Christian organisation which reaches out to people with addiction problems. For over 20 years they ran a residential programme from Ballyards Castle for men with alcohol and drug-related problems.

Dad had a great relationship with the staff and residents. He was a regular speaker at their weekly worship meetings and they often met to pray together. Just by chance, one day, my dad was present when they were chatting that their lease at the castle was coming to an end in 2014. His ears pricked up: this was very interesting to him, as for years my parents had hosted international students in their own home. So my dad thought if he had a castle then he could invite even more!

When Dad heard of their plans, he inevitably began to dream about what could be possible for us in this place. This led the leadership of Drop Inn to once again enter the unknown waiting to hear the voice of God. When Dad shared his heart with the leadership of Stauros and the Ballyards Trust, we began to seek the Lord together.

I still remember the night we all gathered in one of the rooms of the castle. The presence of the Lord was tangible. As a group, there was a sense that Drop Inn could pick up the baton and take responsibility for what God wanted to continue to do in this land. This was confirmed several times from Isaiah 30:21; "*Whether you turn to the left or the right, you will hear a voice behind you saying; 'this is the way, walk in it.*" Shortly after this, we were offered a ten-year lease for Ballyards. The agreement was, we could have it, basically rent free providing we looked after the running and maintenance of the castle.

On 1st April 2015 we moved into Ballyards castle. Before this, Drop Inn was running from the office in my parents' basement. Now today, the castle is like an airport with people coming and going all the time! Confident that the Lord had entrusted us with the keys of the castle, we asked Him for clearer vision in how we could help unlock calling and destiny in the lives of people in Ireland and beyond. We felt Him give us four specific areas.

Ultimately it would be established as a place of prayer: we really want it to be known for the presence of God above anything else. Moreover, after many years of hosting interns at Mum and Dad's home, we were now able to increase the possibilities for our intern programme, which included the running of a three-month mission school as part of their year of training and equipping.

The third area was to offer a place for rest and renewal, for people serving the Lord, however and wherever. We recognised the pain that ministry burnout can cause in a person's life and family, and we wanted to create a safe place for people to get away and experience the presence of God that would refresh and restore. As we continued to seek the Lord, we realised this was a place that would be used to serve the whole body of Christ: a place for Kingdom work. This was not given to build the Drop Inn brand, or serve the Drop Inn vision, but we would hold it open-handed and build Kingdom relationships. Hosting mission teams, organisations conferences became the fourth area of what we felt God was asking us to steward.

The castle became Mum and Dad's new home. From the day they moved in, it has been a constant hive of activity. One group of interns finish their year and another group of young people's experience begins. Local churches and youth groups come in for weekend stays, groups from around the world fly in for week-long retreats, so community living has become their new way of life.

I remember listening to a Brother from a monastery in Northern Ireland say the greatest challenge to the monastic way of life was community living; but the greatest blessing to the monastic way of life was *also* community living. It is this way of life where the 'one anothers' we read about in the Bible are truly lived out. For example, how we live out Romans 12:10; '*Outdo one another in honour*' will be tested while living as a multi-generational, multi-cultural family. Paul writing to the Philippians shows us what becoming more like Jesus looks like; *'Think of others more than yourself, don't look out only for your own interests but the interests of others too, have the same attitude as Jesus.'* Philippians 2:3-5

Establishing a rhythm of prayer becomes essential to the life of a community. Every day before breakfast, morning devotions are shared. Eating together as an extended family is given high priority, so every evening, everyone gathers round the huge dining room table. There are many things that unite people from different parts of the world but we are convinced none more so, than prayer and food!

A contribution from Karolina...

My name is Karolina and I am from Belarus. I was on the internship programme in 2016/2017 and would like to share my personal story of how it impacted me...

Before internship...

I was born into a Christian family and every Sunday I went to church with them. When I was 21-years-old, I felt that God was calling me to do something for Him with my life. I joined the missionary team in my local church. We went to different villages in Belarus and tried to bring the Good News of the Gospel to the people. A few months later, Ronnie Dawson visited my church in Minsk to talk to my pastor about the Drop Inn internship.

When I was told about the opportunity to be part of Drop Inn ministries I felt it was for me, but I was afraid of going to an English speaking country as I couldn't speak English at all! As part of the internship we would go on a missionary trip after completing missionary school. I was excited to get the opportunity to serve in a different country but still I was afraid of having to speak English.

I prayed about it and decided to go to Northern Ireland and take part in the Drop Inn internship.

During internship...

During the first month in Northern Ireland I worked in Drop Inn's charity and coffee shops throughout the day and studied English in the evening. I put a lot of time into learning English, but I still struggled to understand the Northern Irish accent and this made me feel frustrated. One day when I was washing dishes in the Tin House Coffee shop in Portadown, I could hear God asking me; "why do you want to understand what these people are saying more than what I am saying?" The voice sounded so real to me that I stopped doing the dishes and almost began to cry. I answered; "God, I will choose to hear your voice even if I spend a year living here and I cannot understand anyone else." After this experience I stopped worrying about learning English for several hours every day; but other English speakers told me that my English had been improving greatly.

Missionary school

A typical week at missionary school held in the castle looked something like this:

Monday, Wednesday and Thursday – Bible study

Tuesday – As part of the missionary school every Tuesday, Pastor Neil would invite different people to the castle to talk to us about their different ministries.

Friday – Outreach

During missionary school God taught me a lot. One of the most important things that I learned was that God can use anybody for His work.

By the end of the missionary school, God had shown me that He could use me in the same way that He had used those people.

God started to bring me into contact with a handful of Russian speakers through the charity and coffee shops, and we would meet and spend time with each other. Some of these people needed help; this could have been help around the house or help coping with addictions. We spent time with each other, prayed together and talked about God. As time went on, God brought me into contact with more Russian speakers. Before I knew it, I was in contact with 16 Russian speakers, not including children! There were so many that we were able to start having church meetings at the castle once a week. This experience showed me that God could use me even when I did not believe it myself.

Africa...

As part of my internship, I had the opportunity to go on a missionary trip. I prayed about it a lot; Ronnie showed us a list of different countries where we could go. God made me realise that the only place I could go was Burkina Faso in Africa. For two months I helped to build a clinic in Africa and worked as part of a team to run a summer camp. While I was in Africa the people spoke French and Mòoré, I did not speak either of these languages, but this experience taught me that I could show them God's love through actions instead of words.

Working for Drop Inn...

After my trip to Africa ended, I returned to Minsk. I wanted to return to Northern Ireland so that I could continue my work with the Russian speakers, but I did not get the Northern Irish visa I required. At this time, I felt very disappointed because I wanted to serve the Russian speakers in Northern Ireland. However, shortly after this, Ronnie called me and asked me if I wanted to work for Drop Inn and I accepted.

I have been working for Drop Inn for over two years now and I see that God may have closed the door for me in Northern Ireland, but He has opened a much larger door which has led me to doing work in many different countries. I am so thankful to God and Drop Inn Ministries for allowing me to serve so many people around the world.

CHAPTER TWENTY-ONE

Friendships...

Many strong friendships have been formed across the world in 25 years: friends from different nations with similar heart, vision and Kingdom values, who have become family.

Since 2011, Dmitry Shevyakov has been our Eastern European coordinator. We have been blessed working closely with Dmitry and grateful for how he represents the Drop Inn family in Eastern Europe. In recent years, Dmitry has seen a gradual transition in his home country of Belarus as it moves from a state of 'recipient' (of humanitarian aid, doctrinal, financial and missionary support) into the position of 'giver.' We are so encouraged by this, because to receive money from churches in Belarus, Ukraine and Latvia for us to bring to our projects in Burkina Faso and India is such a beautiful expression of the gospel. It reminds me of how Paul was encouraged by the giving of the Macedonian churches and wanted *us to know about the grace God had given them.* He goes on to say; '*In the midst of severe trial, their overflowing joy and their extreme poverty welled up in rich generosity. For I testify that they gave as much as they were able and even beyond their ability. Entirely on their own, they urgently pleaded with us for the privilege of sharing in this service to the Lord's people. And they exceeded our expectations. They gave themselves first of all to the Lord, and then, by the will of God, also to us.'* 2 Corinthians 8:1-5 *NIV*

This giving was never something we made the churches do. Again, as Paul said; *'I'm not commanding you to do this, but I want to see how genuine your love is.'* 2 Corinthians 8:8. Genuine friendship brings real encouragement and life even in the most challenging of times and places. Dmitry highlighted that another helpful shift from recipient to giver has been the knowledge of English among the Christian community in Belarus. He told me: *"To my guess, less than one per cent of church membership could practise English in 2015. We did have a very limited number of skilled Christian interpreters all over Belarus. Since that, year by year, along with the course of Drop Inn internship programme for young people aged 18 to 25, we have seen a lot of progress. In 2015, there were two people on the internship programme and in 2018 and 2019 there were nine young people who spent a year in Northern Ireland with Drop Inn. Nowadays, someone could visit any part of Belarus, east or west, north or south, where a proper number of Christian interpreters (with slight Irish accent over true English) would be at your disposal. Well done, Drop Inn!"*

These friendships have richly enhanced our lives. My parents, my sister and I could never have imagined our lives becoming so intertwined with people from different parts of Ireland, Europe, right to the 'ends of the earth.'

As I think back over the early years in particular, I am so grateful for how Mum and Dad led our family through the changes and challenges of developing an international ministry. I'm glad Mum stayed at home with us (even if a 14-15-year-old Neil might have said otherwise!) while Dad travelled. Even more than that, I am glad, now we have grown up, that she gets to partner more fully with Dad in investing in the lives of our friends around the world. They both carry different graces into each place and situation that complement each other so well. I believe the stories shared through this book testify to that. Nothing was ever forced upon my sister or myself, but we were invited to engage in the journey and we have done that. My sister, Nicola, is just as fully invested into the ministry as I am. She now has four children and works part-time in the Drop Inn office.

And as for me? After seven years of leading church, requests to Mum and Dad for a visit to help and encourage from places all around the world were piling up. After much prayer, they felt it was the right time to pass the leadership of the church to Judith and me. We had already been on the team, and had become increasingly passionate about the church and the local community. We had been living in Craigavon (eight miles from the church) since we got married, but knew we had to make our way back to Richhill. It has been our joy to serve the church and our village ever since.

We changed the name to Grace Community Church, yet we built on the foundation that was laid for us. The values we build on are simple, as in **S.I.M.P.L.E; S**criptures, **I**dentity, **M**issional, **P**resence, **L**ove, **E**veryone, every day, everywhere… We love the **S**criptures, we love that they ultimately point us to Jesus and testify to the birth, life, death, resurrection and ascension of the greatest man who ever lived. Through the words Jesus spoke we discover that if we want to know what the God of the Bible is like, we just need to look at Jesus. John 14:9 is one of the many places

He makes this clear when he tells Philip; *"Anyone who has seen Me has seen the Father."*

As we engage with Scriptures and with our call as *followers of the Way,* we have recognised the need to remind people who they are in Christ, their **I**dentity as sons and daughters of God. Paul is constantly reminding the church of this right through his ministry. With all the crazy things taking place in Corinth, he tells them; *"Anyone who belongs to Christ has become a new person. The old life has gone, a new life has begun."* 2 Corinthians 5:17 *NLT.* In Ephesians 1, before he speaks of anything else, he tells the church who they truly are. In our bibles, there are 12 verses (v3-14) but in its original, it is one long passionate sentence declaring; *'He has loved us;' 'We are chosen in Him;' 'He has adopted us;' 'We are included in Christ.'* We strongly believe that, until we discover who we truly are, all that we are doing is out of duty rather than delight. Once that revelation of *sonship* takes hold of us, we can step into the authority Father has given us; it further develops our understanding of our mission.

A **M**issional life is what God has called all of us to. We have tried to debunk the myth that it's only for professionals; we have tried not to become so reliant on programmes. It is in our workplaces, friendship groups, families, schools etc. where real, everyday life happens. Jesus *'took on flesh and dwelt among us.'* It's this incarnational model of evangelism that we are calling people to. Authentically living out the words and ways of Jesus among those who have yet to truly experience the fullness of His grace, love and peace. Included in the mission of Jesus was time spent with His Father. There were always more people to set free, more places to travel: but for Jesus and for us it can't be at the expense of being in the presence of God.

Jesus continually prioritises **P**resence. One of the many examples is Matthew 14:23; *'After dismissing the crowds, he went up on the mountain by himself to pray. Well into the night, he was there all alone.'* (CSB)

Jesus lived out the instructions for the Kingdom life he preached about in his famous 'sermon on the mount' when He said; *"When you pray, go away by yourself, shut the door behind you and pray to your Father in private."* Matthew 6:6 NLT

We strongly encourage people to live in this rhythm of solitude and service; but we still place high value in our corporate times of prayer, truly believing *'when two or three gather, He is there!'* There is something beautiful when we unite together calling out to God, waiting for His voice, giving space for those prophetic moments that encourage and embolden us.

According to Paul, it is possible to *'give everything to the poor and even sacrifice my body'* and not do it out of love. The One we follow is, most fully described by John; *'God is Love'* and then goes on to say; *'all who live in love, live in God and God lives in them,'* 1 John 4:16. Of all the words that should be used to describe those who follow this God, **L**ove should be high up on the list!

Do the people we spend time with know they are loved?

Do the people in our communities know they are loved?

Do the people we are so tempted to pass judgement on know they are loved?

It's been said that 'we owe people an encounter of Jesus, of love.'

2 Corinthians 5:14 says; *"It is Christ's love that fuels our passion and motivates us, because we are absolutely convinced that he has given his life for ALL of us."* John 3:16 is another reminder of His love for us, so is verse 17. *"God didn't send His Son merely to point an accusing finger telling the world how bad it was. He came to help, to put the world right again."*

As I watch Jesus engage with people in the gospels, I note that before He gave instruction in telling people the way to live, his treatment of them communicated that He was with them, that He was for them. Once people know they are loved, they can trust you to offer direction.

The mission of God, the fulfilling of His plan is for Everyone, Everyday and Everywhere. It is worth quoting Paul's letter to the Ephesians at length here...

'Now grace was given to each one of us according to the measure of Christ's gift. For it says: When he ascended on high, he took the captives captive; he gave gifts to people. But what does "he ascended" mean except that he also descended to the lower parts of the earth? The one who descended is also the one who ascended far above all the heavens, to fill all things. And he himself gave some to be apostles, some prophets, some evangelists, some pastors and teachers, equipping the saints for the work of ministry, to build up the body of Christ, until we all reach unity in the faith

and in the knowledge of God's Son, growing into maturity with a stature measured by Christ's fullness. Then we will no longer be little children, tossed by the waves and blown around by every wind of teaching, by human cunning with cleverness in the techniques of deceit. But speaking the truth in love, let us grow in every way into him who is the head: Christ. From him the whole body, fitted and knitted together by every supporting ligament, promotes the growth of the body for building up itself in love by the proper working of each individual part,' Ephesians 4:7-16 *CSB.* We've all been gifted with something to build up the body of Christ in love, which happens as each does his or her part. I enjoy connecting with other churches because I am realising how much we need each other. I'd delight to see *us all reach unity in the faith* and *growing into maturity* becoming more like Jesus along the way.

In some ways we have come back to where we started. We have rented a small place in the village that we initially opened as a place of prayer, but which now includes a pool table, dartboard and computer games, to connect once again with the young people in our community. Now, 25 years later, the vision to have an outreach to the youth in Richhill is being lived out by the next generation. We read in Acts 1:8, of the Great Commission; *"You will receive power when the Holy Spirit has come on you and you will be my witnesses in Jerusalem, in all Judea and Samaria and to the ends of the earth."* In our context, we have seen that as a call to live a Holy Spirit led life in Richhill, Northern Ireland; and beyond.

There are times I've looked at these verses as a linear process but, after 25 years, I now think it's this ongoing cycle. We took what we had in Richhill seeking to bless our nation and then the world;

now those from the ends of the earth are coming to bless Richhill, our Jerusalem and Northern Ireland, our Judea and Samaria. It sounds **S.I.M.P.L.E!**

CHAPTER TWENTY-TWO

Passing the baton on...

1 Corinthians 4:15; '*There are a lot of people around who can't wait to tell you what you've done wrong, but there aren't many fathers willing to take the time and effort to help you grow up.*' MSG

It is estimated that one generation lasts for 25 years, so we have been asking how does Drop Inn's legacy continue to the next generation? I think, like Paul, we are recognising the need for spiritual mothers and fathers everywhere we are working into. We have many pastors, teachers, cooks, students, who have all been given lots of instructions; but they need mothers and fathers who will take the time and effort to love them, to listen to them and to cheer them on.

As I reflect on the vision David and I had to open Tin House Coffee, I recognise the power of permission. We were allowed to dream, create; and we were also allowed to make mistakes. The power of a father's permission is that a son takes ownership as he is trusted with something. I'm convinced the level of ownership is significant to how well anything is carried into the next generation.

I find it interesting comparing the starfish with a spider. If you were to cut off the head of a spider, it dies, yet if you cut the limb off a starfish it grows right back! There are leaders who lead in such a way that, because they haven't released but held on to everything tightly, what was entrusted to them ceases to exist when they die. Observing various organisations around the world, the spider represents a closed system and the starfish represents an open system. I believe the environment Mum and Dad have created is one of an open system. For example, each year a new group of interns comes to live with them, and there is no hiding place. More responsibility is given to those who are invested; there is an increased level of ownership as authority is distributed.

Over the years, Drop Inn has become more decentralised. We have registered as a charity in Ireland, Isle of Man and North America. We have appointed coordinators who represent Drop Inn among our partners and projects across the world. I think we are trying to find the right balance where there is enough decentralisation for risk and creativity, but enough structure and controls to ensure consistency. I would say Dad is trying to find that right balance between catalyst and CEO.

Drop Inn only exists because Dad is a catalyst. In order to sustain what God has done, Dad has also had to direct and take charge. He has needed to set financial structures in place, create policies and procedures for staff; but we still need the catalyst spirit in him to awaken from time to time. Catalysts are much better at being agents of change than being guardians of tradition. We need to be people who take seriously the responsibility that has been given to us; but we also need to be people caught by the wind of the Spirit,

'*You have no idea where it comes from or where it is headed next,*'
John 3:8 MSG.

The Drop Inn leadership have spent time talking about what
passing the baton on looks like. Whatever it looks like, we want it
to be as healthy as possible. We have witnessed *the baton* being
laid down for someone else to pick up; we have seen the person
handing *the baton* over coming to a stop as they give it to the next
person. But if you are familiar with the relay event in athletics, you
will know that neither of these ways leads to successful transition.
There is a time in the relay when *the baton* is passed from one
member of the team to the other, that they are both running
and holding on to it together. Even when the other person takes
control of *the baton,* the one handing it over doesn't stop straight
away. They might be slowing down, but they are still in the race.

We don't know exactly what our transition will look like, or to
whom it will be entrusted, but I am convinced that its success
will be in Dad running and us holding it together for a time. Even
when it's handed over, maybe running a bit slower, we still need
him in the race. Like Paul said, we need fathers who will cheer us
on! As the writer of Hebrews encouraged us: we want to run the
race marked out for **US**. Hebrews 12:1

Anything God has done, or anything new He is going to do, is
intergenerational. At the birth of the Church, when the Holy
Spirit was poured out, it was on ALL flesh. The young were seeing
visions and the old were dreaming dreams. I love the advice Paul
gives to Timothy in the first letter he writes to him; "*Don't rebuke
an older man harshly but exhort him as if he were your father. Treat*

younger men as brothers, older women as mothers and younger women as sisters." 1 Timothy 5:1-2 MSG

Paul knew that the mission of God was going to be most successful when the family of God, regardless of age or gender, loved and honoured each other well. This is the model we aspire to. Among our shop staff and our partners around the world we have younger men and women being trained and released. Those fathers and mothers who are training and releasing are still in the race with them.

Family on mission...

Within the mystery of the unity of Father, Son and Holy Spirit, there is community, there is family. In the first chapter of Genesis, we read how God began His mission when He created men and women in His image to represent Him. From Adam and Eve, to Abraham, to the journey of the children of Israel, we see the good and bad as we follow the story of family on mission. In the New Testament, we read through the challenges Paul presents to the churches in following the way that reflects the nature of God. I'm convinced that living out the 'one anothers' throughout Paul's letters only makes sense in the context of committed family.

There is a moment in the early stages of Jesus' ministry that we might miss now; it would have shocked those listening to Him. In Mark 3, there is a real buzz of activity around Jesus, the house where he is speaking is full to capacity, and his mother and brothers are outside looking for Him. When Jesus is told this, He responds by asking; *"Who are my mother and brothers?"* And then He looked at those seated in the circle around him and said; *"Here are my mother and brothers! Whoever does God's will is my brother and sister and mother."* (v33-35) With these words, Jesus redefines family. As we follow the gospels and into Paul's letters, we soon realise that the idea of a nuclear family is alien to the scriptures. Jesus has always to be our model in whatever we do. He shows the way in which He is going to fulfil His mission is through extended family.

I appreciate the learning of Mike and Sally Breen, who lead a ministry in Sheffield, England, as they worked out how to be a *family on mission*. They present three options and their consequences;

"Family **OR** Mission crushes us because we have to sacrifice one thing or the other, while both are necessary if we're going to live out the call of God."

"Family **AND** Mission exhausts us because we need to manage the boundaries between family and mission. Thus our family life never quite feels purposeful and our mission never quite feels natural."

"Family **ON** Mission empowers us because we learn to live an integrated life, moving forward in mission as a pack, as a covenant family with a Kingdom mission."

For my sister and me, it feels like we've been family **ON** mission, and we've had the joy of seeing our family extend. Teenage boys and girls became part of our extended family. Shop managers and volunteers became part of our extended family. People across the world, from kids living out in the bush areas of Burkina Faso, to widows in Rwanda, to pastors, wives and kids: all have become part of our extended family.

Our passion is to see the body of Christ in deep fellowship with one another, and on a mission to love God, love one another and to love the world with the love of Christ as an ordinary family of God on mission. We really don't want mission to be another programme or project; we don't want visits around the world to just fill the calendar. I don't think discipleship or mission fully works until we understand we are family.

As I think of the races, genders, ages, cultures and denominations that make up our ever-increasing family, I am always reminded of what Paul said in Galatians 3:28; *"There is neither Jew or Greek, neither slave or free, nor is there male or female for you are ALL ONE in Christ Jesus."*

One of my favourite chapters in the Bible is Romans 8. In it we are reminded who we truly are… sons and daughters of Father God! Paul goes on to say; "Now if we are children, then we are heirs – heirs of God and co-heirs with Christ." NIV

God is our Father, Jesus is our older brother. We are a family on mission and the truth is we are not doing mission **FOR** God, we are doing mission **WITH** Him!

So as for *this* Family on Mission: we look forward to what new challenges and blessings God has in store for us and for the generations to follow.

'Declare His glory among the nations, His marvellous deeds among all peoples. For great is the Lord and most worthy of praise.' Psalm 96:3-4

Father, we thank you for all you have done among your people across the world. We thank you for every person who has contributed, whether staff, volunteers or donors, who has allowed us to bless your people in spiritual and practical ways. We thank you for every part of this Drop Inn family' who continue boldly and faithfully to serve their communities, laying down their lives for the sake of the gospel.

'Now to Him who is able to do immeasurably more than we can ask or imagine according to the power that is at work within us. To Him be glory in the church and in Christ Jesus throughout all generations for ever and ever! Amen.' Ephesians 3:20-21

Be part of our family…

It would take more than one book to fully tell the story of our extended family, but I pray you have felt our heart; and more so, the heart of God that we seek to emulate.

We would love you to become part of our family and help us continue our work at home and internationally. Our shops always need more stock, our managers always need more volunteers. Or why not come and join us on one of our mission trips?

The story is not over, and you can do your part, whether sponsoring a child, a programme, (training, food, care etc.) medical, evangelism, pastoral care, etc.

Why don't you drop us a line? We would love to hear from you!

Contact us at the following:

Drop Inn HQ
Ballyards Castle
123 Keady Road
Armagh
BT60 3AD
T. ++44 (0) 28 3778 9406

E. info@dropinn.net
Facebook: www.facebook.com/DropInnHQ/

www.DropInn.net

FAMILY COMMENTS

"Cooperation with Drop Inn has been a great blessing to me for many years now. I value this relationship and thank the Lord for it. Cooperation with Drop Inn inspires me to serve the Lord in all circumstances of life. Drop Inn family is a support and inspiration for me. Thanks to our cooperation, I have many opportunities to bring the Gospel to various people through various ministries. Relationships in Drop Inn family are especially dear for me: I have made many friends in different countries with whom we have established close relations and new ministries. Prayers for each other are very precious and it is worth so much."
Sergey, Pridnestrovie

"By their own life, Ronnie and Carolyn teach me far more than anybody else around me to get the one million or more inspirations I need under my belt to serve people around me. I do appreciate it!"
Dima, Belarus

"The investment Drop Inn has put into me is being expressed to others, many of whom Drop Inn has never personally met. Drop Inn's influence goes far beyond what their eyes can see. Along our pilgrimage through this world, God arranges a few key people to come into our lives. For us, among those few key people, Ronnie and Carolyn were and still are significant."
Eugene, Canada

"Ronnie is a man of simplicity and humility; his wife Carolyn is a woman who is always filled with the joy of the Lord. My team and I have been amazingly blessed through their lives about whose investment the heaven will greatly testify on the Last Day."
Stephen, South India

"We are extremely grateful for the faithfulness of Drop Inn over all these years, as without their very important contribution to the work, LAM would not have been able to accomplish all that has been done so far. We would like to congratulate them on their 25 years of wonderful, fruitful ministry all over the world!"
Sandra, Brazil

"It is their love for people and how it moves them into action that is so admirable and a true mark of Ronnie and Carolyn's walk with God and their love for Him."
Paul, Turkey

"I pray blessings on Ronnie, Carolyn and family. God bless you in your immensely great cause for the Lord."
Gregoriy, Ukraine

"Ronnie and Carolyn have not only been amazing supporters of GOC, but amazing friends that we can share our hearts and burdens."
Lindita, Albania

"To work together with Drop Inn has impacted and shaped Solace Ministries in a special way. The approach of partnership based on mutual trust is so inspiring."
Jean, Rwanda

"Pastor Ronnie has a great heart for our nation to do God's work. I always got inspired when I saw his face; which always showed a smile."
Emmanuel, Pakistan

"As a family we were struggling financially. In answer to our prayer, the Lord connected us to Drop Inn. Since then, they have been lovingly supporting us in the work of the ministry for which we're forever grateful to God and thankful to Drop Inn for their strong partnership."
Reuben, India/Nepal

"Each person from the Drop Inn family has left a very good mark on my memory and I am very grateful for them."
Gena, Latvia

"We are grateful to God for the love he has lavished upon us and we continue to appreciate the paths of service through Drop Inn Ministries."
Paul, Kenya

"As a missionary serving with Drop Inn Ministries, I have seen first-hand the impact that the ministry has had on multitudes of people in many countries of the world. I am thankful to God for the lives of Ronnie & Carolyn as they continue to extend 'help, hope and healing' (in Christ's name) to the nations."
Nigel, Venezuela

"Lois and I would like to congratulate Ronnie and Carolyn on reaching twenty-five years of a wonderful ministry, ten of which has been the support and encouragement to our schools and teachers at Drop Inn ministries, Zambia. Thank you both; and may you have good health to continue the wonderful work. God bless you."
Robert and Lois, Zambia

"To me, Drop Inn has been and still is God's true channel of great blessings to the hopeless people in the world. Through Drop Inn, many eastern European hopeless children's needs were graciously met. In 2003, Drop Inn was led by God our Father to sincerely save many hopeless orphans in Koudougou, Burkina Faso. When you are related to Drop Inn, there is hope in life. Drop Inn is God's true instrument to bring hope to a broken world."
Etienne, Burkina Faso

INSPIRED TO WRITE A BOOK?

Contact
Maurice Wylie Media
Inspirational Christian Publisher

Based in Northern Ireland and distributing around the world.

www.MauriceWylieMedia.com